Entrepreneur.
VOICES

ON

EMOTIONAL INTELLIGENCE

The Staff of Entrepreneur Media, Inc.

Entrepreneur Press®

Entrepreneur Press, Publisher
Cover Design: Andrew Welyczko
Production and Composition: Eliot House Productions

Library of Congress Cataloging-in-Publication Data
    Names: Small, Jonathan J., editor. | Entrepreneur Media, Inc.
    Title: Entrepreneur voices on emotional intelligence / by the staff
        of Entrepreneur Media, Inc.; edited by Jonathan Small.
    Description: Irvine, California: Entrepreneur Media, Inc., [2018] |
        Includes bibliographical references.
    Identifiers: LCCN 2018022895| ISBN 978-1-59918-635-1 (alk.
        paper) | ISBN 1-59918-635-7 (alk. paper)
    Subjects: LCSH: Emotional intelligence. | Entrepreneurship—
        Psychological aspects. | Businesspeople—Psychology.
    Classification: LCC BF576 .E58 2018 | DDC 152.4—dc23
    LC record available at https://lccn.loc.gov/2018022895

Printed in the United States of America
22 21 20 19   10 9 8 7 6 5 4 3 2 1

CONTENTS

PART II
PERCEIVING OTHERS

PART III
COPING AS AN ENTREPRENEUR

Contents

PART IV

MAINTAINING YOUR EQ

FOREWORD BY LEWIS HOWES

The New York Times *Bestselling Author,*
Top 100 Podcast, www.lewishowes.com

Being a leader in today's world is very similar and very different from being a leader in times past. In some ways, timeless leadership principles still apply. In other ways, leaders today are expected to be masters of far more skills than ever before. Emotional intelligence is one of those skills that is required but often overlooked, misunderstood, or just ignored. While it is a skill that has always been present in the great leaders of history, today it is something we can openly discuss and study. That is why this book was written—to support the modern-day leaders of business in understanding and living up to their full potential as leaders of human beings. It starts with self-awareness and moves into awareness of others in a powerful and enlightening way.

I was already successful in business, influence, and athletics before I was ever introduced to the idea of emotional intelligence. On the outside, it looked like I had my life and relationships figured out. But in fact, I came to study this skill as a result of some of my worst choices in my relationships. Not only did I realize that I was helpless when I was triggered emotionally, I knew that I had to learn how to understand what was happening inside of me if I wanted to reach my full potential. Through workshops, coaching, mentors, and a lot of practice, emotional intelligence has become one of my most prized skills. I still work on it every day, but the more I learn and apply my findings, the more at peace I become as a person, the more effective I become as a leader, and the better all of my relationships, both business and personal, become.

In fact, studying and applying the principles of emotional intelligence led me to write a book on the masks men wear to avoid showing their emotions. If you had told me six years ago that I would be writing a mainstream book on that topic, I would have been terrified. Only through doing the work of emotional intelligence myself did I find the courage to speak up about how lost I had been when it came to my emotions before.

I'm guessing you picked up this book because you too are a seeker. You're someone who is interested in becoming the very best version of yourself, and you know you have work to do to get there. You may be curious about what other entrepreneurs have to say on this subject. Or you might realize that a mirror to your own inner self can be found by reading the experiences of others. You are right. Investing in learning about how your emotions are triggered, how you respond, and how others are affected by your response is a life-changing decision. Take it from someone whose entire life changed as a result of studying this topic.

Whatever made you pick up this book, I am convinced that if you honestly take in the wisdom offered by these entrepreneurial voices, your relationship with yourself, your team, your business, and your future will transform dramatically. These thought leaders (many of whom I know personally and have learned from myself) are walking the talk when it comes to their self-awareness, relationships, and leadership. You'll have to work hard to find a better collection of wisdom on this topic, especially coming from business owners who have walked the path towards emotional intelligence themselves.

I invite you to open your mind (and heart) wide as you read these stories, insights, and lessons. Let yourself see the reflection of your own strengths and weaknesses as you read their words. Be willing to get uncomfortable, honest, and curious about yourself. What is available to you on the other side is more than a new kind of intelligence—it's freedom to be the best version of yourself.

THE ONE TALENT YOU DIDN'T KNOW YOU NEEDED

In his landmark 1990 bestseller, *Emotional Intelligence: Why It Can Matter More Than IQ*, journalist Daniel Goleman popularized a revolutionary theory that had been bouncing around academic circles for years: Having a high IQ is not the be all end all. There is another kind of intelligence, "emotional intelligence" or EQ, that is even more instrumental in helping you succeed in business and in life.

Goleman wrote, "If you don't have self-awareness, if you are not able to manage your distressing emotions, if you can't have empathy and have effective relationships, then no matter how smart you are, you are not going to get very far."

Brain and behavioral research has confirmed this. A landmark 1970s study by the Carnegie Institute of Technology showed that 85 percent of our financial success was due to skills related to emotional intelligence, while only 15 percent had to do with technical skill. That historical data bears out over time. For example, 20 years later in the late 1990s, search firm Egon Zehnder International studied 515 executives and found that those who had high EQ were more likely to succeed.

So we know EQ is important, but what is it, exactly? Simply put—emotional intelligence is the ability to recognize and manage your own emotions and the emotions of others. High EQers all share a number of key traits. Number one on the list is self-awareness. They trust their feelings on everything from which employees to hire to what lunch to order. People with emotional intelligence also have greater self-control. They don't throw temper tantrums or allow bad news to throw them off course. Instead, they know how to manage their emotions and soothe their fears and anxiety.

Emotionally intelligent people are not only kind to themselves, but they're also empathetic to others. They are able to motivate those around them by appealing to their better nature. Think of the last time a salesperson convinced you to buy a car or upgrade your phone plan. Was it because he scared you into it or because she convinced you it was the right thing to do? People with solid EQs excel at interpersonal skills and likability.

How do you become more emotionally intelligent? You can start by reading this book. Inside is a collection of useful articles penned by experts and entrepreneurs on strategies to boost your EQ. The book is broken down into four sections—Awareness, Perception, Coping, and Maintenance—each designed to help you nurture and develop the various facets of emotional intelligence. Spoiler alert: EQ takes work and practice. Some of us are naturally born with it, but most of us need to consistently nurture and develop it.

ACHIEVING SELF-AWARENESS

re you self-aware? According to a 2017 study of executives, 95 percent think they are. They believe they understand everything they need to know about their behavior and their emotions. There's only one problem with this perception—it isn't true. In her book, *Insight: How Small Gains in Self-Awareness*

Can Help You Win Big at Work or in Life, psychologist Tasha Eurich says the number of business leaders who are actually self-aware is closer to 10 to 15 percent, according to her research. "It can be problematic," she said in a recent podcast interview. "A lot of times, the people who have the most room to improve are the least likely to know."

Problematic is right. Strong self-awareness is one of the pillars of emotional intelligence. The more we are aware of our emotions, the more control we have other them. This is not only good for us; it's good for business. A 2017 study conducted by The Potential Project of 1,000 leaders in more than 800 companies found that leaders at the highest levels tend to have better self-awareness than leaders lower in the hierarchy.

To better understand how to increase our self-awareness, you first have to know what it is. Dr. Eurich divides it into two categories of knowledge. The first is what we commonly associate with the term—being introspective and aware of our own behavior and emotions and understanding our values and aspirations. The second type of self-awareness, she says, is knowing what other people think of you. Those who "have both types of self-knowledge and balance them are the ones who are the most successful at work and in life," says Dr. Eurich.

Self-awareness helps you make smart decisions. It leads to empathy and kindness. People who are self-aware are not afraid to show vulnerability and authenticity. They're much less likely to fly off the handle in moments of stress, get defensive, or blame others for their shortcomings. Lawrence A. Bossidy, the former CEO of AlliedSignal, says, "Self-awareness gives you the capacity to learn from your mistakes as well as your successes. It enables you to keep growing."

The following chapters help you develop your self-awareness by identifying the traits and signs of entrepreneurs who possess a healthy dose of EQ. You'll learn the importance of understanding your strengths and weaknesses, nurturing healthy and trusting relationships with your co-workers, believing in yourself, and being a good judge of character. On the flip side, you'll also learn about the habits of the woefully *un*self-aware. People who hold grudges can't let go of mistakes and have no idea what their triggers are or how to regulate them. Hopefully, by being more aware of whether or not you're self-aware, you'll fall more in the 10- to 15-percent bracket and less in the 80 percent who are lying to themselves.

WHAT IS EMOTIONAL INTELLIGENCE AND WHY DOES IT MATTER?

Gerard Adams

Most people are conditioned to believe that knowledge is power when, in fact, knowledge is only potential power. In my life, I've been blessed enough to have many meaningful conversations, yet the one I had on emotional intelligence with a young woman, Ashley Zahabian, who I met at the entrepreneurial incubator that I recently launched, Fownders, really resonated with me.

We were going through her pitch deck and stumbled across the topic of "EQ" (emotional intelligence). As the conversation grew more in depth, she told me a powerful story of a young boy and his grandfather that truly altered my perception.

"A young boy and his grandfather were sitting in a car on their way to a restaurant to grab dinner," she said. She went on explaining how the grandfather was curious as to what his grandson's choice of food would be.

"Salmon! I love salmon so much," the little boy shouted with high energy.

The grandfather stayed quiet as they pulled up to the restaurant and parked their car to go inside. About twenty minutes later, the food finally arrives and the little boy devours his meal and enjoys every bite of his favorite food. The grandfather, a little uneasy, approaches his grandson with a critical question.

"So you love fish, huh?" he asked.

"I do! My favorite part is the crunchy end! Thank you so much, Grandpa," the little boy shares.

Instead of appreciating the thanks from his grandson, however, the grandfather continues to question the little boy.

"Grandson, I want you to understand what I've become aware of over time. Thirty minutes ago, you told me how much you loved that fish, and how it was your favorite fish ever. I want you to think about something, though. In order to eat that fish, do you know what that fish went through? First, there was a hook that made the fish bleed and feel pain. Second, it was taken away from its family. Third, it was killed. Then, it was burned so you can enjoy that extra crisp. Last, it was chewed up by you so you can taste the deliciousness of a grilled piece of salmon. Grandson, are you sure you love the fish, or do you just love yourself?" The little boy's grandfather continued, "In life, Grandson, everything is built on relationships, but this is what kills them. We claim to love people or want to do well for those around us but continue to do what's best for ourselves. That's not love; that's called selfishness."

He closed the conversation by teaching his grandson what it meant to become self-aware of the words we choose, decisions we make, and emotions we are truly feeling; he taught his grandson how self-awareness could service him in learning how to serve those he claimed to love.

"You want a good life, little man?" asked the grandfather.

"Sure do, Grandpa," the little boy responded.

"Then here is the secret: when you learn to control and take care of your emotions, you learn to focus on everybody else because you're already taken care of. When you can focus on everybody else, you learn how to serve them. When you learn to serve them, you then deserve them… and if you can deserve them, the relationships will make your life a successful one."

The little boy felt disappointed in himself after realizing his grandfather was right until his grandfather told him that this was a life-long lesson that was well worth the slip-up. The little boy then smiled with appreciation and felt grateful that it all happened.

Powerful story, right? Well, what I learned from this was that whether we like it or not, emotions will fuel our every decision. Even when we have the most logical facts in front of us, the deciding variable is our emotional response. If we can't control that response, we will keep eating the fish we love and damaging the relationships that make up our life and happiness.

The form of self-awareness that the grandfather was teaching his grandson is called emotional intelligence. Emotional intelligence is the capacity to practice self-awareness to better understand ourselves and thus become more compassionate and conscious toward the experiences of others. The discussion around emotional intelligence and its value has grown over the past few years.

Currently, most of society and the traditional educational system is consumed with the traditional style of teaching that entails memorization of facts and testing. However, the setback with this kind of education is that it merely accounts for our academics. To add to this, we can't consistently increase our IQ throughout our life within this limited scope of knowledge and awareness. In comparison, our emotional intelligence infiltrates our relationships, our health, our diet, our management style, our wealth or lack of it, our parenting style, and every other aspect of our lives; it can continually be improved, which is why investing in emotional intelligence and self-awareness is a huge advantage.

Try asking yourself: What would you rather invest in, a car or a home? The wise decision would be a home because the ROI (return on investment) on a home is positive, whereas a car drops in fiscal value over time. Understanding that our time is more valuable than our bank account, wouldn't you want your time to have a high ROI as well? You can either spend years investing in IQ, which won't return much progressive change, or your EQ, which can return a much grander margin of progressive and consistent change.

This reason alone is why I've begun paying more attention to my emotional intelligence—I can control it.

Another great advantage to investing in your emotional intelligence is the power to expand your happiness. At some point in life, everybody experiences life's struggle that take us on the high-low emotional roller-coaster. Emotional intelligence allows us to become aware of the lesson rather than the surface level pain. Just like the little boy who felt disappointed after he slipped up; once his grandfather expressed that this would be a life-long lesson worth the mistake, the little boy felt immediately content and appreciative. At the end of the day, our mission in life is growth. When we are able to invite growth, the pleasure overrides the pain, and we become happier individuals. IQ, on the other hand, cannot create this happiness.

The list of benefits for emotional intelligence goes on; it is the only consistent way to instill happiness and confidence in ourselves, and it teaches us to serve the world authentically.

Ashley shared with me that she continues to ask herself before every decision she makes, "Am I loving the fish or myself right now?" I recommend that we all ask ourselves the same question and for every aspiring entrepreneur to invest in emotional intelligence. After that, the journey is a fun ride.

2

11 SIGNS THAT YOU LACK EMOTIONAL INTELLIGENCE

Travis Bradberry

When emotional intelligence (EQ) first appeared to the masses, it served as the missing link in a peculiar finding: people with average IQs outperform those with the highest IQs 70 percent of the time. This anomaly threw a massive wrench into the broadly held assumption that IQ was the sole source of success.

Decades of research now point to emotional intelligence as being the critical factor that sets star performers apart from the rest of the pack. The connection is so strong that 90 percent of top performers have high emotional intelligence.

Former chairman and CEO of General Electric Jack Welch says, "No doubt emotional intelligence is more rare than book smarts, but my experience says it is actually more important in the making of a leader. You just can't ignore it."

Emotional intelligence is the "something" in each of us that is a bit intangible. It affects how we manage behavior, navigate social complexities, and make personal decisions to achieve positive results.

Despite the significance of EQ, its intangible nature makes it very difficult to know how much you have and what you can do to improve if you're lacking. You can always take a scientifically validated test, such as the one that comes with the book *emotional intelligence 2.0*.

Unfortunately, quality (scientifically valid) EQ tests aren't free. So, I've analyzed the data from the million-plus people TalentSmart has tested in order to identify the behaviors that are the hallmarks of a low EQ. These are the behaviors that you want to eliminate from your repertoire.

You get stressed easily.

When you stuff your feelings, they quickly build into the uncomfortable sensations of tension, stress, and anxiety. Unaddressed emotions strain the mind and body. Your emotional intelligence and coping skills help make stress more manageable by enabling you to spot and tackle tough situations before things escalate.

People who fail to use their emotional intelligence skills are more likely to turn to other, less effective means of managing their moods. They are twice as likely to experience anxiety, depression, substance abuse, and even thoughts of suicide.

You have difficulty asserting yourself.

People with high EQs balance good manners, empathy, and kindness with the ability to assert themselves and establish boundaries. This tactful combination is ideal for handling conflict. When most people are crossed, they default to passive or aggressive behavior. Emotionally intelligent people remain balanced and assertive by steering themselves away from unfiltered emotional reactions. This enables them to neutralize difficult and toxic people without creating enemies.

You have a limited emotional vocabulary.

All people experience emotions, but it is a select few who can accurately identify them as they occur. Our research shows that only 36 percent of people can do this, which is problematic because unlabeled emotions often go misunderstood, leading to irrational choices and counterproductive actions. People with high EQs master their emotions because they understand them, and they use an extensive vocabulary of feelings to do so. While many people might describe themselves as simply feeling "bad," emotionally intelligent people can pinpoint whether they feel "irritable," "frustrated," "downtrodden," or "anxious." The more specific your word choice, the better insight you have into exactly how you are feeling, what caused it, and what you should do about it.

You make assumptions quickly and defend them vehemently.

People who lack EQ form an opinion quickly and then succumb to confirmation bias, meaning they gather evidence that supports their opinion and ignore any evidence to the contrary. More often than not, they argue, ad nauseam, to support it. This is especially dangerous for leaders, as their under-thought-out ideas become the entire team's strategy. Emotionally intelligent people let their thoughts marinate because they know that initial reactions are driven by emotions. They give their thoughts time to develop and consider the possible consequences and counter-arguments. Then, they communicate their developed idea in the most effective way possible, taking into account the needs and opinions of their audience.

You hold grudges.

The negative emotions that come with holding on to a grudge are actually a stress response. Just thinking about the event sends your body into fight-or-flight mode, a survival mechanism that forces you to stand up and fight or run for the hills when faced with a threat. When a threat is imminent, this reaction is essential to your survival, but when a threat is ancient history, holding on to that stress wreaks havoc on your body and can have devastating health consequences over time. In fact, researchers at Emory University have shown that holding on to stress contributes to high blood pressure and heart disease. Holding on to a grudge means you're holding on to stress, and emotionally intelligent people know to avoid this at all costs. Letting go of a grudge not only makes you feel better now but can also improve your health.

You don't let go of mistakes.

Emotionally intelligent people distance themselves from their mistakes, but they do so without forgetting them. By keeping their mistakes at a safe distance, yet still handy enough to refer to, they are able to adapt and adjust for future success. It takes refined self-awareness to walk this tightrope between dwelling and remembering. Dwelling too long on your mistakes makes you anxious and gun shy, while forgetting about them completely makes you bound to repeat them. The key to balance lies in your ability to transform failures into nuggets of improvement. This creates the tendency to get right back up every time you fall down.

You often feel misunderstood.

When you lack emotional intelligence, it's hard to understand how you come across to others. You feel misunderstood because you don't deliver your message in a way that people can understand. Even with practice, emotionally intelligent people know that they don't communicate every idea perfectly. They catch on when people don't understand what they are saying, adjust their approach, and re-communicate their idea in a way that can be understood.

You don't know your triggers.

Everyone has triggers—situations and people that push their buttons and cause them to act impulsively.

Emotionally intelligent people study their triggers and use this knowledge to sidestep situations and people before they get the best of them.

You don't get angry.

Emotional intelligence is not about being nice; it's about managing your emotions to achieve the best possible outcomes. Sometimes this means showing people that you're upset, sad, or frustrated. Constantly masking your emotions with happiness and positivity isn't genuine or productive. Emotionally intelligent people employ negative and positive emotions intentionally in the appropriate situations.

You blame other people for how they make you feel.

Emotions come from within. It's tempting to attribute how you feel to the actions of others, but *you* must take responsibility for your emotions. No one can make you feel anything that you don't want to. Thinking otherwise only holds you back.

You're easily offended.

If you have a firm grasp of who you are, it's difficult for someone to say or do something that gets your goat. Emotionally intelligent people are self-confident and open-minded, which create a pretty thick skin. You may even poke fun at yourself or let other people make jokes about you because you can mentally draw the line between humor and degradation.

Bringing It All Together

Unlike your IQ, your EQ is highly malleable. As you train your brain by repeatedly practicing new emotionally intelligent behaviors, it builds the pathways needed to make them into habits. As your brain reinforces the use of these new behaviors, the connections supporting old, destructive behaviors die off. Before long, you begin responding to your surroundings with emotional intelligence without even having to think about it.

THE IMPORTANCE OF EMOTIONAL INTELLIGENCE IN THE WORKPLACE

Mariah DeLeon

Scholars may have coined the term "emotional intelligence" in the early 1990s, but business leaders quickly took the concept and made it their own.

According to emotional intelligence, or EQ, success is strongly influenced by personal qualities such as perseverance, self-control, and skill in getting along with others. Much has been written about how to improve employees' EQ, but hiring managers are likely to make better hiring decisions when they look for people who already possess high EQ scores.

At Glassdoor, we see our 2,100 employer clients like Zillow and 1-800-CONTACTS working hard to better connect with both employees and job seekers. Why? Because they know that in order to keep their culture intact and to effectively recruit the right kind of candidates, they need to engage and be open and transparent.

Workers with high EQ are better able to work in teams, adjust to change, and be flexible. No matter how many degrees or other on-paper qualifications a person has, if he or she doesn't have certain emotional qualities, he or she is unlikely to succeed. As the workplace continues to evolve, making room for new technologies and innovations, these qualities may become increasingly important.

In his books, *emotional intelligence: Why It Can Matter More than IQ* and *Working With emotional intelligence*, Daniel Goleman presents five categories of emotional intelligence. To hire candidates who will thrive in your workplace, look for those who have a handle on these five pillars:

1. *Self-awareness*. If a person has a healthy sense of self-awareness, he understands his own strengths and weaknesses as well as how his actions affect others. A person who is

self-aware is usually better able to handle and learn from constructive criticism than one who is not.

2. *Self-regulation*. A person with a high EQ can maturely reveal her emotions and exercise restraint when needed. Instead of squelching her feelings, she expresses them with restraint and control.

3. *Motivation*. Emotionally intelligent people are self-motivated. They're not motivated simply by money or a title. They are usually resilient and optimistic when they encounter disappointment and driven by an inner ambition.

4. *Empathy*. A person who has empathy has compassion and an understanding of human nature that allows him to connect with other people on an emotional level. The ability to empathize allows a person to provide great service and respond genuinely to others' concerns.

5. *People skills*. People who are emotionally intelligent are able to build rapport and trust quickly with others on their teams. They avoid power struggles and backstabbing. They usually enjoy other people and have the respect of others around them.

Just as it's important to seek new hires with emotional intelligence, it's vital for managers and other business leaders to operate in emotionally intelligent ways to meet the needs of today's workers.

Many older workers started their careers at the same companies from which they retired. A job, for many in older generations, was viewed simply as a vehicle for earning an income. Today, however, most workers want more from their jobs than simply a paycheck. Younger generations have seen that the traditional view didn't always work out as they've watched their loyal older counterparts deal with rampant layoffs and workplace disappointments.

While the emotional needs of today's workforce may seem like a tall order for employers, they're worth your attention. Investing in EQ has brought our company more engaged, committed employees, and we'll continue to put a premium on this effort moving forward.

4

ARE YOU SELF-AWARE? FIVE KEY TRAITS TO BE A GREAT ENTREPRENEUR

Jonathan Long

Entrepreneurial success stories are few and far between. Only 30 percent of businesses survive a decade, according to the Bureau of Labor Statistics' Business Employment Dynamics.

Chris Cavallini, the founder and CEO of national meal-service company Nutrition Solutions, has done more than just build a business that can survive. Nutrition Solutions does more than $10 million in annual revenue, and their clients include

NFL player Rob Gronkowski and WWE world heavyweight champion Jinder Mahal.

I met with Cavallini, and we talked about the keys to successful brand-building. One thing that Cavallini kept circling back to was self-awareness. That discussion led to us breaking down self-awareness into five parts, which I have highlighted below and think all entrepreneurs can benefit from.

Operate with a Give-First Mentality

Cavallini struggled with business relationships in the beginning, which he attributes to having a difficult childhood and parents who did not build an empowering home. He focused on what people owed him and what he could get from them, which he eventually realized was the wrong approach. This attitude was negatively affecting his relationships, so he started focusing on how he could create value for others.

The "give-first" mentality is something that I have personally used throughout my entrepreneurial journey, and it's led to valuable personal connections, business ventures, and amazing opportunities.

When you shift your perspective, you can see—and experience—massive changes in your life. Instead of expecting others to give to you, look for ways to help others, even if it's just with words of encouragement or advice. Donating to charities and helping people outside of his work environment are two things that Cavallini feels are extremely important.

Don't Expect Anything in Return

If you start a business expecting to build a wildly successful company or become filthy rich, it will often lead to disappointment. Chase your dreams, and the success and money will often follow.

When you remove expectations from the equation, it allows you to spend more time and energy focusing on the things that truly matter. The focus and dedication required to be successful comes when you truly love what you do.

Treat People Like Family

Cavallini did not have strong family relationships growing up, forcing him to take care of himself. You never understand the importance of having a support system, set of advisors, or friends until you are in a time of need.

This relates to a very important point when it comes to entrepreneurship—do your due diligence when it comes to hiring. Some founders rush to make hires simply to fill roles, while others hire and then never interact with their employees again.

It's important to take the time to nurture the relationships within your company. Your team will always perform better when they feel appreciated and part of something bigger than themselves. Create a team environment and treat everyone as you would your family.

Believe in Yourself First

"I don't think anyone I grew up with expected me to do the things I'm doing today, and I can't blame them for that because back then I didn't even believe in myself. The moment I started to see my potential, the faster I grew," said Cavallini.

It sounds cliché, but it's true—you have to believe in yourself before you can expect anyone else to get behind you. Cavallini takes this mentality a step further and adds the importance of nurturing that self-confidence over time. It's not something that happens immediately. For him, it came during the years spent in the gym—that's where he found himself. That self-confidence was leveraged, allowing him to transition into entrepreneurship.

Write Down Your Goals

Write your goals down in detail and look at them every day. Break down your entire large goal into several micro-goals to help improve your chances of success. This allows you to see progress and remain motivated, even in difficult times.

Writing down goals is nothing new to entrepreneurs, but Cavallini offers a slight variation. He recommends writing goals down in the past tense, as if they've already happened. This strategy helped him believe he was capable of accomplishing what he set out to do.

If you ever feel down or unmotivated, go back to your goals for inspiration. Write them down in a notebook that is always by your side, or put them on a whiteboard that you are constantly looking at.

By practicing these five strategies on a regular basis, you will develop a greater capacity to be self-aware that impacts not only your business success but your own peace of mind. When you know who you are and what makes you tick, you take that power out of someone else's hands and control your own destiny.

FIVE SIGNS YOU'RE TOO EMOTIONAL TO DECIDE WHAT'S BEST FOR YOUR BUSINESS

Jayson DeMers

Decision making is one of the biggest responsibilities of an entrepreneur or business owner.

You're in charge of determining the strategic direction for the business, hiring people, coordinating plans, and responding to changes and crises as they emerge. Because businesses are logical, numbers-driven organizations, your decisions need to be as logical as possible if you want to succeed.

The problem is, it's hard to remain completely logical when making decisions in a business you're emotionally invested in. You're going to feel sentimental attachments and have emotional reactions to events, but it's important to prevent these feelings from obscuring your logical decision making processes.

Keep an eye out for the following signs that your emotions are clouding your ability to make grounded, sensible decisions.

1. You consider personal relationships.

Personal relationships can be important, especially in a startup environment when you're working with a small team.

You need to know how your teammates work with and engage with one another, and you need to be on friendly terms with them to keep morale high. However, if your personal relationships start dominating your decision making, it could spell eventual trouble for your organization.

For example, let's say you have an employee who has become a close personal friend of yours, but this employee has been failing to meet your expectations when it comes to productivity and contributions. Your personal attachments to him or her may prevent you from making the right decision and firing him or her, which could cause harm to your organization.

2. You hold tightly onto your own ideas.

It's natural to treat your ideas with a bit of favoritism, but it's easy for this tendency to balloon into something that's not only illogical but also straight-up counterproductive.

For example, if you come up with a new idea for a sales strategy that you're especially proud of, you might become overly attached to it once you put it into action.

If you don't see results from it, you might rationalize that it's because it hasn't been given a long enough time to take effect, or you might use alternative data points to support its existence. Try to look at the data from an outside perspective, as objectively as possible, to compensate for this. Trust the numbers.

3. You bounce back and forth on your position.

Do you ever find yourself going back and forth excessively on a decision? If you're facing a truly difficult decision, with legitimate merits and drawbacks to both sides, this is natural.

However, it could be an indication that your emotions are influencing your position. For example, if you feel especially exhausted or pessimistic, you might lean toward a safer, easier option. On the other hand, if you feel excited or optimistic, you might lean toward a riskier one with a higher potential payoff. Consider what you're feeling and how those feelings are affecting your switchbacks.

4. You can't identify why you made a decision.

This is a retrospective strategy, but it's one of the most important ones on this list. Think back to the last decision you made, and try to summarize why you made that decision in a sentence or two.

You can also apply this to a decision you're about to make by justifying why you're making this decision. If your answer is, "I don't know," or if it takes you a while to find a logical justification, it could be because your decision was driven by emotion.

5. Other people don't understand your rationale.

Don't misinterpret this; you don't need to rely on other people to make your decisions. In fact, going with what other people think or recommend will eventually compromise your vision as an entrepreneur. However, it's often valuable to learn what other people think about your decision options as doing so can open you up to new, alternative perspectives.

If you start explaining your latest decision to other people, and none of them understand your line of reasoning, it could be because you're influenced by emotions, which a person removed from the situation doesn't have. Think carefully about what's really influencing you, and see if you can pinpoint an emotion that's driving that rationale.

None of this is to say that emotions shouldn't play any part in your decision making process. In fact, if you made decisions based only on logic, with no emotion whatsoever, you'd become robotic, and you'd miss out on some of the greatest advantages of the human mind like instinct and creativity.

The key is to not let your emotions rule or dominate your logical side. Emotions can serve as influencers for your decisions so long as they're recognized for what they are and you keep them in check. Keep this in mind as you continue your entrepreneurial journey and make even more impactful decisions for your business.

WHY VULNERABILITY, AUTHENTICITY, AND LOVE ARE THREE MUST-HAVES

Mary Deelsnyder

It takes a lot of characteristics to run a business. Ambition, intelligence, and tenacity are just a few. It also takes love—love of your vision, your work, and yourself. Love is the thing that burns inside you when people tell you that you should give up on your idea. It's the reason you get out of bed in the morning, ready to kick butt at your own business. Love is also the grace you grant yourself when you make a big mistake.

Love can take many forms, like showing vulnerability by putting yourself out there, trusting in a process to allow something to unfold, and being authentic with the people you encounter every day. It can seem uncomfortable to talk about these things in a business, but the truth is, that's where all the magic happens.

I was lucky to speak with four entrepreneurs about love and business. The women that I spoke with expressed a lot of love for the work they do. They were honest with me about that, and it was very inspiring. Below are excerpts from our conversations, and I'm certain you will share similarities to the stories that these women tell.

Shantell Martin is a visual artist based in New York and California. She made a business out of her art six years ago because she wanted to be in control of her creations. When she moved to New York City, she quickly faced the possibility that being a working artist may not happen. She was challenged by the art business model and found that it wasn't set up to work in the artist's favor. So, like a true entrepreneur, she created her own business model and took galleries out of the equation.

I was most compelled by two things that Shantell talked about. When I asked her how she discovered her style, she said that she didn't really discover it.

She just kept drawing over and over—and her style unfolded in front of her. She trusted the process—the guide to what was already inside of her.

That's a lesson that you won't learn in business school. We all have what we need inside of us—we just need to be brave and patient in order to let it be free.

The second takeaway from our conversation was the idea that mindset can change everything. Being an artist is not an easy career choice. It can be a long road of rejection, self-doubt, and financial challenges. While Shantell was in the middle of a struggle, a friend asked her: "Has it occurred to you that you don't need to struggle?" That simple question shifted things for Shantell because she started to imagine what life would be like if she was a successful artist. It set her on a path of success that she continues to enjoy today.

Jahan Mantin and Boyuan Gao of Project Inkblot exhibit the kind of authenticity that make you want to be their best friend. "We want to feel like we belong" is what inspired the start of Project Inkblot. Even though women of color were featured in the media, it's how they were spoken to that felt inauthentic to Jahan and Boyuan. They think that it's important for women and communities of color to tell their own stories in their own authentic voices.

Their company creates cross-cultural campaigns and develops experiential workshops and mission-based cultural programming (just to name a few of their services). They do this work so they can ensure that under-served communities have a seat at the table. They've had early success in their business. It's easy to understand why when you speak to them in person. They are unwavering and laser-focused on their mission. Their authenticity translates to everything they do, even the tough business challenges.

They shared a story with me about being too eager to work on a new project and entered into an agreement with the client without doing their due diligence. As the project moved along, they found themselves miserable because things weren't going the way they should. They took responsibility for their role in the matter and, instead of being miserable anymore, saw the situation for what it was—an opportunity for a deeper connection to the work and their client.

They decided to be honest and express their concerns with their client. They were coming from a place of shared commitment for the success of the campaign, so they had the right approach. The conversation wasn't easy, but it was necessary. Once they spoke candidly with their client, the project went smoothly and turned out to be one of their biggest success stories.

Sometimes we need to remember to have compassion for people, even our clients. Sitting down face-to-face with someone and respectfully communicating with them can solve a lot of problems. Slow down and do this—it will impact your business and your life.

Lynne McDaniel owns An Orange Moon, a vintage interior furnishings and design center. She sells mid-century modern designs.

Lynne grew up in an entrepreneurial family and has that unique combination of business savvy and creativity. She learned a lot about design while growing up because her mother was a graduate of Vogue College of Design in Chicago. Weekends were spent going to design shows, art museums, and the flea market on Maxwell Street (so her dad could hunt for vintage tools).

Lynne was bitten by the design bug early and started collecting vintage items at a very young age. She's turned her love of design into a thriving furniture business and feels like she has created a fairytale life. She also believes that anyone can have the life they want. You just have to make that choice, work hard, and keep moving forward. Success is a mindset, and it's her genuine wish that everyone could understand that.

After speaking with these four impressive entrepreneurs, I learned that we all go through similar challenges as business owners and as women. The special thing about women, though, is our ability to put ourselves out there as only women can. With that comes great power and responsibility, so trust the process, be authentic, and always lead with love.

SEVEN SIGNS THAT YOU'RE AN EMOTIONALLY INTELLIGENT PERSON

Jayson DeMers

Emotional intelligence is an underrated quality for entrepreneurs and a crucial one for employees. Simply put, it's your ability to recognize and control your emotions and to recognize and understand the emotions of others.

But why is this quality important, and how can you tell if you have it?

Why is Emotional Intelligence Important for Entrepreneurs?

People with high emotional intelligence are good at reading people, navigating and understanding their own feelings, and interacting with others. These are just four of the most important areas where emotional intelligence can help:

- *Stability.* If you want to lead a team of employees—or manage a community of followers—you need to remain emotionally stable, even in times of crisis. Emotional intelligence helps you control anger, panic, and despair and remain calm no matter what.
- *Sales and service.* Understanding what people feel, why they feel it, and what they want or need is pivotal if you want to sell products and services that people really want. It can also help you close deals once the businesses gains momentum.
- *Motivation.* Being able to relate to your employees and understand their feelings boosts morale and motivates those staffers to become more successful in your environment.
- *Mediation and negotiation.* Emotional intelligence also helps you resolve conflicts between and among employees or partners and gives you an advantage when you're attempting to negotiate.

Signs of emotional intelligence

So, how can you tell if you yourself are emotionally intelligent? Look for these signs:

1. *You're able to articulate emotional experiences.* We're taught emotional vocabulary basics as young children with words like happy, sad, silly, and mad. But how articulate are you at describing your more complex emotional experiences? An expressive and precise vocabulary is a sign that you're introspective enough to understand your own emotions— and how emotions work in general. For example, you might describe something as "nostalgic" rather than "a little sad," or feel "stress-related irritability" rather than "anger."

2. *You can pinpoint strengths and weaknesses easily (including yours).* Emotionally intelligent bosses are able to quickly discover their employees' strengths and weaknesses—and aren't afraid to admit their own. Everyone is good at different things, and everyone has personal shortcomings. Ferreting these out is a sign that you pay close attention to how people interact and you see both the bad and good in people.

3. *You've historically been a good judge of character.* Think about the other people you've interacted

with in the past, whether they're former team members or friends. When you had a "good feeling" about someone, how did your relationship with them turn out?

First impressions can be deceiving, but if you have a strong history of choosing reliable, trustworthy and positive people to surround yourself with, you probably have a strong ability to judge people's character.

4. *People come to you for advice or support.* How often do people in your life come to you for advice when they're facing a tough problem? Or support when they're going through a hard time? If lots of people do, that means they trust you not to judge them, and you probably give them valuable emotional perspective.

In other words, it's a sign that you're an emotionally intelligent person and that other people can see that.

5. *You can let things go.* All leaders experience moments of frustration, irritation, and anger, but how quickly are you able to move past yours? Are you the type of person who holds onto grudges or the type who forgives and forgets? Do your mistakes haunt you, or do you try to work past them as quickly as possible?

Emotionally intelligent people are able to control their reactions and let things go with relative ease.

6. *You generally know how others are feeling.* Can you tell when your top employee is especially stressed out, even when he or she isn't explicitly acting like it? Do you notice when your friends are acting strangely, even if that activity is only slightly different from their usual behavior?

Only emotionally intelligent people notice these differences consistently.

7. *You accept other beliefs, work styles, and perspectives.* There's no one "right" type of professional; there are dozens, if not hundreds, of acceptable beliefs, work styles and perspectives. Are you the type of person who accepts and embraces them? Or do you try to convert everyone to your specific style?

If you don't think you exhibit these signs, don't worry. Some people are naturally inclined to be more emotionally intelligent than others, but it's a skill and an awareness that can be developed over time. Start by paying more attention to the thoughts, feelings, and behaviors of the people around you, and make it a point to talk to strangers.

The more you focus on others' wants, needs, and perspectives, the more you'll learn about the human condition, and the better you'll become as a leader.

8

EMBRACE THE IMPERFECT PICTURE BENEATH YOUR MASTERPIECE

Ray Hennessey

Behind Mona Lisa's smile, there may be another view entirely: a woman looking straight ahead, with a neutral stare, perhaps even a frown of disappointment. At least that's what one French researcher is suggesting, though art historians aren't so sure.

It's common for artists to paint over existing canvases. Picasso's famous *The Blue Room* was actually painted over another work of an unidentified man in a bowtie. Reduce, reuse, and recycle, I guess.

But we paint over our hidden pictures, too. Each of us.

What is beneath your portrait?

Very few of us are truly authentic. I'm not. I try to be, but in small ways, I'm not. My Facebook posts don't have pictures of when I argue with my spouse. Many people erase photos of exes from their social-media posts the moment the relationships fall apart. Our LinkedIn pages don't mention the reasons we were fired. People who spend half their Internet time watching porn prefer to tweet out *Daily Show* clips instead.

We live a sanitized authenticity, a perfect picture—not only on social media but also in person. Look around your office environments. Many people are cheerily going about their day. But these same folks are people struggling with real demons. Addicts. People suffering from mental illness. Cheaters. Thieves.

You never see the darkness these people have. There are two reasons for that. First, we don't want to. We want to frame the people closest to us in the way that best suits our field of vision. Life is a symphony that needs are constantly conducting, and there is no room for discordant notes.

Second, people by their nature put the positive above the negative in their appearance—physical, emotional, and psychological. They need to, both to interact effectively with folks around them and to cope with the problems they have.

Yet, we have to understand that there is another picture hidden under everyone's portrait, especially our own.

Some of our hidden pictures are simply abandoned or aborted. We started out wanting to do something else—wanting to be someone else—and we just decided that isn't the path we could follow. There is no shame in that. We tried something. It didn't work. We moved on.

In other cases, the picture underneath us was simply unfinished. Life takes us many directions, and it often means we are forced to prioritize things differently. Business leaders, in particular, live in a world charged with demands—for our time, our attention, our love, our emotion. Things that were once important to us sometimes fall away. We intend to return to them but often can't.

Lastly, we consciously abandon some of our inner pictures. These are the paths we travel down, personally and professionally, that we need to stop doing. Divorces. Bad habits. For business leaders and entrepreneurs, it's the failures we are bound to encounter.

It takes a lot to see these hidden pictures. In the case of the Mona Lisa, it took a technique called Layer Amplification Method, according to the BBC, which measures the reflection of light to reconstruct images between layers of paint.

But if they can be measured in any way, these pictures are real. Our inner pictures may not be visible to the eyes of others, but they, at a minimum, provide a different texture to the portrait we present to the world. We need to embrace that and understand it in order to move forward. If we have conquered depression, we don't need to share that with our co-workers and partners, but we certainly have to make sure that accomplishment is a layer of paint in the lives we choose to lead. If we've failed, we have to take comfort knowing the canvas was sturdy enough to bear a better piece of work. If we were once a man in a bowtie, we have to be comfortable being a woman in a room of blue.

We can't take joy in our accomplishments if we've never been tested. We are defined by a combination of the challenges we choose to face, the setbacks laid at our feet, and the manner in which we tackle all of those. Each is a brushstroke, a layer of paint that sometimes resonates but more often needs to be covered by another color, shade, or texture. The good news is that the result, from a masterpiece to

Dogs Playing Poker to a child's watercolor, is always a unique, important piece of work, the fruit of our conscious, intentional labor, and commitment.

Life and art are interchangeable, and as Thomas Merton wrote, art "enables us to find ourselves and lose ourselves at the same time." It would have been tragic had the world not had Mona Lisa and her smile. It would be equally tragic if the world didn't have you, the way you face it. But we cannot forget the pictures we can't easily see. Instead, we need to embrace the foundation they provide. If you're successful, you will never look at your own portrait the same way again.

ENTREPRENEUR VOICES SPOTLIGHT: INTERVIEW WITH HARVEY DEUTSCHENDORF

Author and Emotional Intelligence Researcher

Harvey Deutschendorf has earned the nickname "E.I. Guy" for his extensive work researching on and lecturing about emotional intelligence. Born into a poverty-stricken immigrant family, he was the first to graduate from college and "make it" in their adopted country of Canada. But despite his business success, Deutschendorf felt something was missing. He had his answer when he discovered Daniel Goleman's book, *emotional intelligence*. His life's work became understanding and developing his emotional intelligence and sharing his discoveries with others.

His book, *The Other Kind of Smart: Simple Ways to Boost Your emotional intelligence for Greater Personal Effectiveness and Success*, offers readers the tools needed to nurture emotional intelligence Deutschendorf also lectures frequently on the topic. To take his EI Quiz, go to http://theotherkindofsmart.com/ei-quiz.

Entrepreneur: What was it about emotional intelligence that made such an impact on you?

Deutschendorf: After reading Goleman's book, it just struck me that this was the answer. My emotions were the problem regardless of how high my IQ was. I need to control and manage my emotions—make them work for me instead of against me. And so I wrote a book explaining what emotional intelligence is and how we can change it because unlike IQ, which is mainly set for the rest of our lives, emotional intelligence can be changed.

Entrepreneur: What are some of the hidden barriers we construct that limit our potential?

Deutschendorf: One of the essential barriers to overcome is the thought "You can't do this," or "You're not able to do this." With my background, it was ingrained in my mind all the time that I wasn't capable of, say, being an author because people in my family didn't do things like this. Once I became aware of these thoughts, I began to challenge them. At first, it was scary and very frightening because you have to go out of your comfort zone. Your comfort zone will keep you safe, but it will also keep you small. You won't try things that you're probably able to do but are afraid to do. By challenging yourself, you work towards realizing your potential.

Entrepreneur: You wrote that there's one significant obstruction that limits our potential. What is it?

Deutschendorf: Fear. Most people will choose comfort over discomfort. But the people who become successful are willing to be uncomfortable; they are eager to feel and face fear—to keep pushing ahead, even when they're afraid. I try to do things consistently that challenge my fears. For example, I'm now working on doing a TEDx Talk. It's very exciting. But it's also scary. But I will not let fear stop me. That's my mantra. I will not let fear stop me.

Entrepreneur: How much of emotional intelligence is being able to manage our emotions?

Deutschendorf: When something comes into our brain, it goes into the emotional part first—the amygdala. And if we don't give ourselves time to think it over and react, it can be catastrophic. The worst example of not being able to manage our emotions is road rage. There are hundreds of deaths in the U.S. every year due to road rage. And that's a case of again where we feel before we think.

Entrepreneur: So, what have you done to manage your own emotions?

Deutschendorf: If I get an intense emotion, instead of reacting, I will start counting. I'll count to ten. And by the time I've counted to six or seven, I'm not liable to react in a highly emotional way. I give myself a timeout. I've calmed down and started to think. The frontal cortex has kicked in.

PART I
ACHIEVING SELF-AWARENESS—REFLECTIONS

Emotional intelligence starts with a strong sense of self-awareness. Because entrepreneurs with high EQ's know their strengths and weaknesses, they're able to manage their emotions rather than let their emotions manage them. And they exhibit self-confidence and open-mindedness that is infectious to those around them.

People who lack self-awareness are more likely to have a low EQ, which manifests itself as stress, insecurity, and an inability to understand how you come across to others. Those who are unsure of themselves are unsure of the decisions they make. When others question their judgment, the self-*un*aware tend to get defensive and angry—they hold grudges and surround themselves only with people who agree with them.

As we practice being more aware of our behavior and how it affects those around us, we develop a stronger sense of who we are. This leads us to make better decisions, have more self-control, and ultimately be more successful in work and in life.

PERCEIVING OTHERS

Think of emotional intelligence as a bit of a superpower. Not only does it infuse you with a sense of inner confidence and control, but it also enables you to perceive the behavior of others better. Superman had X-ray vision. Emotionally intelligent people have *E-ray* vision—they can see the emotions of those around them.

While those with high EQs are not mind-readers, they're skilled at reading body language and the unspoken signals that others send—both positive and negative. For example, they realize that the simple act of crossing your arms or legs telegraphs that you're not open to what someone else is saying. You might not even be aware that your clenched jaw is indicating stress, but an emotionally intelligent person is on to you. They can recognize a real smile from a fake one. They read facial expressions more adeptly, sensing worry, fear, or dishonesty even if the person is trying to project the opposite emotion.

People with high EQ are also skilled at reading personality types. They can determine if a person is an introvert or an extrovert, insecure or confident, closed- or open-minded. This is helpful when you're negotiating with someone or trying to determine if you should negotiate with them in the first place.

Because emotionally intelligent people are in control of their own emotions, they are better able to help others control their own emotions. They have a knack for calming down fellow employees who are feeling anxious and stressed. They know how to turn a mindset of doom and gloom into a more optimistic one.

None of this would be possible without the ability to plug into others and see what makes them tick. This section of the book helps you identify and hone your perception powers.

FOUR WAYS TO TAME YOUR NEGATIVITY BIAS

Anis Qizilbash

When I began speaking publicly and delivering workshops, there always seemed to be one audience member who looked disengaged. Despite the other 30+ happy and enthusiastic delegates, my mind fixated on that single seemingly unhappy person. Inevitably, I'd start to doubt myself, which affected my performance.

In the face of so many good things to be happy about, why does our brain obsess over the negative?

Humans Are Hardwired for Danger

According to *Personality and Social Psychology Review*, when two events of equal objective magnitude take place, you feel the bad event more forcefully, pervasively, and enduringly than the good event.

This negativity bias served the evolution of humans thousands of years ago, helping us respond to imminent threats like a dangerous animal.

In the *Review of General Psychology*, Baumeister, Bratslavsky, Vohs, and Finkenauer say, "A person who ignores the possibility of a positive outcome may later experience significant regret [...], but nothing directly terrible is likely to result. In contrast, a person who ignores danger [...] even once may end up maimed or dead."

We're not in that kind of danger anymore, but our brain still operates primally, reacting disproportionately to those things we perceive as "negative."

Fight-or-Flight Hijacks Creativity and Productivity

The brain is complex, but there are two bits of grey matter that are central to this discussion. The prefrontal cortex is in charge of brain functions that are critical to business success, including things like empathy, creativity, and problem-solving. Then there's the amygdala, a key player in our emotional development. It's also known as the fear center.

Since the amygdala sits closer to the brainstem than the prefrontal cortex, it rapidly transforms stimuli into signals, alerting the body to threats. Your body obeys the warning, triggering an increase in heart rate, a shortening of breath, and tension throughout the body. Furthermore, when the amygdala is triggered, some functions of the prefrontal cortex shut down, eliminating unnecessary brain activity to conserve energy.

As entrepreneurs, we have to make decisions, prioritize, and solve problems every day; essentially, we get paid to think. But the science shows that if we operate from primal states of fear and scarcity, we are not operating optimally.

Stop Getting Carried Away by Negative Thoughts

Negative thoughts and emotions are like a juggernaut tearing down a highway. You're not going to stop them with an emergency handbrake maneuver. You need to slow them down first. There is a way of rewiring our instinctive negative bias.

After regular mindfulness meditation practice, the amygdala quiets down and actually shrinks while the prefrontal cortex thickens. Like building your upper body with push-ups, you can increase your emotional balance and tame your fear response with regular practice.

Tame Your Brain's Negativity Bias

Here are four simple steps you can practice to reduce anxiety, maintain your calm, and operate from an empowered state.

1. Get Present

During a three-minute break in the workshop mentioned earlier, I paid attention to my hands to anchor myself to the present moment. When you catch yourself in an unproductive or agitated state, pay attention to your sense perceptions. Be aware of your hand on your lap or your foot in your shoe. Some days you might barely register a vague tingle while other days it might seem like your hand is vibrating. This simple mindfulness practice can be done anywhere, and doing so takes attention away from thoughts and brings you into the present.

2. Detach from Your Thoughts

Next, you want to be aware of thoughts without getting carried away by them like a runaway train. Observing your thoughts creates detachment. You can do this by asking yourself, "What am I thinking? What is the conversation in my head?" Repeat this a few times.

In the workshop above, I told myself the audience member was not enjoying himself. In his book *Mindsight: The New Science of Personal Transformation*, Dr. Dan Siegel says naming an emotional affect soothes firing of the emotional center. Or in other words, "Name it to tame it."

3. Challenge the Thought

Perhaps that one audience member wasn't unhappy. Or perhaps it was just his resting face.

According to *Learned Optimism: How to Change Your Mind and Your Life*, challenging negative thoughts can reduce the emotional intensity and eventually eliminate feelings of panic. So ask yourself "Is that thought really true, right now in this moment? What is the likelihood of that really happening?"

4. Crowd Out Negative Thoughts

Finally, to shift yourself to an empowered state, ask yourself what you are grateful for. I reminded myself that everyone else in the workshop was having fun and that even though that one audience member looked unhappy, he was doing the exercises so he was probably engaged.

Invest the next two minutes listing the things you're grateful for in your business and why you're grateful for each one. Flooding your mind with thoughts of gratitude crowds out negative thoughts.

Next time you see an email, news headline, or something that triggers your negativity bias, get yourself present, detach from the thought, challenge the thought, and ask yourself what you are grateful for that day. This process will shift you to a more empowered state. Practice regularly, and you will eventually tame your brain's negativity bias, allowing you to operate in a more optimal manner and unleash your creativity.

10

CUT PEOPLE A BREAK. YOU NEVER KNOW WHAT THEY'RE GOING THROUGH.

Jim Joseph

When I go through the toughest times of my life, I never let people know. I just put my head down and plow ahead. And while I'm never one to complain or say that I have it bad, I have dealt with my fair share of struggles through managing personal relationships, raising two kids, and addressing financial burdens—sometimes all at once.

I never let people in, though, during those times because I have never wanted anyone to judge me or think that I was weak. I'm not saying that this is the way to handle your own life, but it is the way that I've chosen to handle mine. For better or worse . . .

As a result, in my darkest hours, people around me still treated me the same way. They still expected the same cheerful, optimistic, over-achieving, and hyper-productive Jim. There was no room for a frown, an excuse, or a mistake. I preferred it that way, but even I must admit that every once in a while, I wish someone had cut me a break. There were days I didn't feel like smiling, didn't feel like being positive, and didn't feel like producing.

But I put my head down and plowed ahead no matter what.

It was my fault. Those around me had come to expect certain things of me, and I gave them no indication that they should expect otherwise in the moment. How could I not deliver unless I explained why?

Sure, each situation and burden soon passed only to be met with a new challenge—but then again, that is life. Life is about learning from our experiences, so what did I learn from these struggles?

I should probably learn to come clean and let people in. But honestly, I don't always want to, and we each have our reasons for handling our own situations. We each have our ways of dealing with issues. That's not my lesson learned.

What I learned instead is that we should cut people a break.

All of us are going through something at any given time. While we might not talk about it, that doesn't mean it's not there and that it's not causing real impact.

So, cut people a break.

If they seem a little less patient one day, let it go. If their normally perfect work product is a little less than perfect once in a while, then fix it for them. If they snap at you and cut you off multiple times in a row, roll with it. Maybe they're going through something difficult and just can't live up to their own standards in that moment. Maybe there's something else going on that is getting in their way right now. Maybe something else is up.

Cut them a break.

There is no need to say anything; nor is there need to make it a big deal. They might not even notice—and perhaps that's exactly what they need. Perhaps they just need someone to let it slide this one time, someone to turn the other way and not make it a big deal.

This is what I've learned.

We have no idea what people are going through at any given moment, so cut them a break when perhaps they need it most. I would have appreciated it through the years.

NINE SIGNS YOU'RE DEALING WITH AN EMOTIONAL MANIPULATOR

Travis Bradberry

We all know what it feels like to be emotionally manipulated. It can be extremely effective, which is why some unscrupulous individuals do it so much.

A few years ago, Facebook, in conjunction with researchers from Cornell and the University of California, conducted an experiment in which they intentionally played with the emotions of 689,000 users by manipulating their feeds so that some users only saw negative stories while others only saw positive stories. Sure enough, when these people posted their own updates, they were greatly influenced by the mood of the posts they'd been shown.

Facebook caught a lot of flak over the experiment, primarily because none of the "participants" gave their consent to join the study. Perhaps more frightening than Facebook's faux pas was just how easily people's emotions were manipulated. After all, if Facebook can manipulate your emotions just by tweaking your newsfeed, imagine how much easier this is for a real, live person who knows your weaknesses and triggers. A skilled emotional manipulator can destroy your self-esteem and even make you question your sanity.

It's precisely because emotional manipulation can be so destructive that it's important for you to recognize it in your own life. It's not as easy as you might think because emotional manipulators are typically very skillful. They start out with subtle manipulation and raise the stakes over time so slowly that you don't even realize it's happening. Fortunately, emotional manipulators are easy enough to spot if you know what to look for.

1. *They undermine your faith in your grasp of reality.* Emotional manipulators are incredibly

skilled liars. They insist an incident didn't happen when it did, and they insist they did or said something when they didn't. The trouble is they're so good at it that you end up questioning your own sanity. To insist that whatever caused the problem is a figment of your imagination is an extremely powerful way of getting out of trouble.

2. *Their actions don't match their words.* Emotional manipulators will tell you what you want to hear, but their actions are another story. They pledge their support, but when it comes time to follow through, they act as though your requests are entirely unreasonable. They tell you how lucky they are to know you and then act as though you're a burden. This is just another way of undermining your belief in your own sanity. They make you question reality as you see it and mold your perception according to what is convenient to them.

3. *They are experts at doling out guilt.* Emotional manipulators are masters at leveraging your guilt to their advantage. If you bring up something that's bothering you, they make you feel guilty for mentioning it. If you don't, they make you feel guilty for keeping it to yourself and stewing on it. When you're dealing with

emotional manipulators, whatever you do is wrong, and no matter what problems the two of you are having, they're your fault.

4. *They claim the role of the victim.* When it comes to emotional manipulators, nothing is ever their fault. No matter what they do—or fail to do—it's someone else's fault. Someone else made them do it—and, usually, it's you. If you get mad or upset, it's your fault for having unreasonable expectations; if they get mad, it's your fault for upsetting them. Emotional manipulators don't take accountability for anything.

5. *They are too much, too soon.* Whether it's a personal relationship or a business relationship, emotional manipulators always seem to skip a few steps. They share too much too soon— and expect the same from you. They portray vulnerability and sensitivity, but it's a ruse. The charade is intended to make you feel "special" for being let into their inner circle, but it's also intended to make you feel not just sorry for them but also responsible for their feelings.

6. *They are an emotional black hole.* Whatever emotional manipulators are feeling, they're geniuses at sucking everyone around them

into those emotions. If they're in a bad mood, everyone around them knows it. But that's not the worst part: they're so skillful that not only is everyone aware of their mood, they feel it, too. This creates a tendency for people to feel responsible for the manipulator's moods and obliged to fix them.

7. *They eagerly agree to help—and maybe even volunteer—then act like a martyr.* An initial eagerness to help swiftly morphs into sighs, groans, and suggestions that whatever they agreed to do is a huge burden. And if you shine a spotlight on that reluctance, they'll turn it around on you, assuring you that, of course, they want to help and that you're just being paranoid. The goal? To make you feel guilty, indebted, and maybe even crazy.

8. *They always one-up you.* No matter what problems you may have, emotional manipulators have it worse. They undermine the legitimacy of your complaints by reminding you that their problems are more serious. The message? You have no reason to complain, so shut the heck up.

9. *They know all your buttons and don't hesitate to push them.* Emotional manipulators know your weak spots, and they're quick to use

that knowledge against you. If you're insecure about your weight, they comment on what you eat or the way your clothes fit; if you're worried about an upcoming presentation, they point out how intimidating and judgmental the attendees are. Their awareness of your emotions is off the charts, but they use it to manipulate you and not to make you feel better.

Overcoming Manipulation

Emotional manipulators drive you crazy because their behavior is so irrational. Make no mistake about it—their behavior truly goes against reason, so why do you allow yourself to respond to them emotionally and get sucked into the mix?

The more irrational and off-base someone is, the easier it should be for you to remove yourself from their traps. Quit trying to beat them at their own game. Distance yourself from them emotionally, and approach your interactions with them like they're a science project (or you're their shrink, if you prefer that analogy). You don't need to respond to the emotional chaos—only the facts.

Maintaining an emotional distance requires awareness. You can't stop someone from pushing your buttons if you don't recognize when it's happening.

Sometimes you'll find yourself in situations where you'll need to regroup and choose the best way forward. This is fine, and you shouldn't be afraid to buy yourself some time to do so.

Most people feel as though because they work or live with someone, they have no way to control the chaos. This couldn't be further from the truth. Once you've identified a manipulator, you'll begin to find their behavior more predictable and easier to understand. This will equip you to think rationally about when and where you have to put up with them and when and where you don't. You can establish boundaries, but you'll have to do so consciously and proactively. If you let things happen naturally, you're bound to find yourself constantly embroiled in difficult conversations. If you set boundaries and decide when and where you'll engage a difficult person, you can control much of the chaos. The only trick is to stick to your guns and keep boundaries in place when the person tries to cross them, which they will.

Bringing It All Together

Emotional manipulators can undermine your sense of who you are and even make you doubt your own sanity. Remember: Nobody can manipulate you without your consent and cooperation.

12

EIGHT GREAT TRICKS FOR READING PEOPLE'S BODY LANGUAGE

Travis Bradberry

Body language provides an amazing amount of information on what other people are thinking if you know what to look for. And who hasn't wanted to read people's minds at some point?

You already pick up on more body language cues than you're consciously aware of. UCLA research has shown that only seven percent of communication is based on the actual words we say. As for the rest, 38 percent comes from tone of voice, and the remaining 55 percent comes from body language. Learning how to become aware of and to interpret that 55 percent can give you a leg up with other people.

When you're working hard and doing all you can to achieve your goals, anything that can give you an edge is powerful and will streamline your path to success.

TalentSmart has tested more than a million people and found that the upper echelons of top performance are filled with people who are high in emotional intelligence (90 percent of top performers, to be exact). These people know the power that unspoken signals have in communication, and they monitor body language accordingly.

Watch Your Cues

Next time you're in a meeting (or even on a date or playing with your kids), watch for these cues:

- *Crossed arms and legs signal resistance to your ideas.* Crossed arms and legs are physical barriers that suggest the other person is not open to what you're saying. Even if they're smiling and engaged in a pleasant conversation, their body language tells the story. Gerard I.

Nierenberg and Henry H. Calero videotaped more than 2,000 negotiations for a book they wrote on reading body language, and not a single one ended in an agreement when one of the parties had their legs crossed while negotiating. Psychologically, crossed legs or arms signal that a person is mentally, emotionally, and physically blocked off from what's in front of them. It's not intentional, which is why it's so revealing.

- *Real smiles crinkle the eyes.* When it comes to smiling, the mouth can lie, but the eyes can't. Genuine smiles reach the eyes, crinkling the skin to create crow's feet around them. People often smile to hide what they're really thinking and feeling, so the next time you want to know if someone's smile is genuine, look for crinkles at the corners of their eyes. If they aren't there, that smile is hiding something.

- *Copying your body language is a good thing.* Have you ever been in a meeting with someone and noticed that every time you cross or uncross your legs, they do the same? Or perhaps they lean their head the same way as yours when you're talking? That's actually a good sign. Mirroring body language is something we do unconsciously when we feel a bond with the other person. It's a sign that the conversation is going well and that the other party is receptive to your message. This knowledge can be especially useful when you're negotiating because it shows you what the other person is really thinking about the deal.

- *Posture tells the story.* Have you ever seen a person walk into a room and, immediately, you have known that they were the one in charge? That effect is largely about body language and often includes an erect posture, gestures made with the palms facing down, and open and expansive gestures in general. The brain is hardwired to equate power with the amount of space people take up. Standing up straight with your shoulders back is a power position; it appears to maximize the amount of space you fill. Slouching, on the other hand, is the result of collapsing your form; it appears to take up less space and projects less power. Maintaining good posture commands respect and promotes engagement, whether you're a leader or not.

- *Eyes that lie.* Most of us probably grew up hearing, "Look me in the eye when you talk to me!" Our parents were operating under the assumption that it's tough to hold someone's gaze when you're lying to them, and they were right to an extent. But that's such common knowledge that people will often deliberately hold eye contact in an attempt to cover up the fact that they're lying. The problem is that most of them overcompensate and hold eye contact to the point that it feels uncomfortable. On average, Americans hold eye contact for seven to ten seconds, longer when we're listening than when we're talking. If you're talking with someone whose stare is making you squirm—especially if they're very still and unblinking—something is up and they might be lying you.

- *Raised eyebrows signal discomfort.* There are three main emotions that make your eyebrows go up: surprise, worry, and fear. Try raising your eyebrows when you're having a relaxed casual conversation with a friend. It's hard to do, isn't it? If somebody who is talking to you raises their eyebrows and the topic isn't one that would logically cause surprise, worry, or fear, there is something else going on.

- *Exaggerated nodding signals anxiety about approval.* When you're telling someone something and they nod excessively, this means that they are worried about what you think of them or that you doubt their ability to follow your instructions.

- *A clenched jaw signals stress.* A clenched jaw, a tightened neck, or a furrowed brow are all signs of stress. Regardless of what the person is saying, these are signs of considerable discomfort. The conversation might be delving into something they're anxious about, or their mind might be elsewhere and they're focusing on the thing that's stressing them out. The key is to watch for that mismatch between what the person says and what their tense body language is telling you.

Bringing It All Together

The bottom line is that even if you can't read a person's exact thoughts, you can learn a lot from their body language, and that's especially true when words and body language don't match.

THE NEW EMOTIONAL WORKPLACE AFFECTS HIRING, RETENTION, AND CULTURE

Jason Wesbecher

Do you want to attract and retain top performers? It might be time to start looking more closely at how you foster relationships. Candidates are driving the job market, and they are increasingly making professional decisions based on emotional compatibility with their prospective employer. In fact, according to a 2016 survey by Mattersight of American office workers, positive emotional connections and work relationships are no longer just a luxury for employees and job seekers—they're a necessity. This priority on relationships is forcing employers to rethink their strategic approach to hiring, candidate retention, and growing corporate culture. Relying on emotional intelligence factors and personality data are driving the American workplace to become a new emotional workplace.

Applying the Science of Personality and Emotion

Survey data shows that compensation alone is no longer enough of a singular selling point for top performers and job candidates. There needs to be a promise of connection and autonomy coupled with responsibility on behalf of the employer to identify what can be controlled and improved when problems arise. When asked to rank the top three reasons they look for a new job, employees cite friction with managers, poor internal communication, and lack of empowerment via workplace/cultural policies. The theme of problems arising through *strained relationships* can be heard loud and clear.

So how can employers guarantee solid relationships between employees and a collaborative, productive work environment? Getting actionable insights, like the business world has grown so accustomed to, out of these three pillars may seem like a daunting task. But there is one critical, though often overlooked, tool employers *can* employ: personality data.

If used properly, personality data gives the employees extremely valuable insight into their colleagues, managers into their reports, and executives into their companies as a whole. This allows employers to rethink their strategic approach to hiring, candidate retention, and growing corporate culture for lasting success.

Personality assessments that are built to hone in on an employee's work style, examining workplace motivators, triggers, etc. comprise a valuable first step for gaining insights into employees. Taking an analytical look into these traits can make it easier to implement a meaningful, proven strategy for improving the emotional intelligence, corporate culture, and bottom line of a brand. Here are a few ways this data can be used to a business' advantage.

Foster Company-Wide Respect

Employers need to understand their employees unique work style, habits, and environmental needs. Taking into account how employees derive satisfaction and view accomplishments on the job will go a long way as not everyone translates achievement, success, or failure in the same way. With personality data, you can parse out how each personality style responds to a spectrum of job factors and use that data to inform business structure and build a better emotional workplace.

Restructure Teams Based on Personality and Work Style

Don't forget to think about how you can help employees build strong relationships with colleagues. Top performers place a lot of value on having a cohesive team that works well together and understands each other's needs. Making sure they are matched with peers who balance their style or jive well—even if they're a different personality type—will increase productivity for individuals and teams and mitigate avoidable job snafus.

Differentiate Between Management Style and Preference

Train managers to know and take into account how each of their direct reports works best, and acknowledge the differences. Place importance on matching the right mentee with the right mentor. Having a strong rapport with their boss and/or supervisors will make employees more satisfied and lead to better business outcomes for all involved.

Define Employee Retention by Emotional Connection

Fifty percent of American office workers have stayed at an unsatisfying job because of positive emotional relationships. Conversely, 65 percent say they would look for a new job because of poor internal communication. The unifying factor in both of these responses is the importance connections played for workers. It's a strong indicator that companies need to rethink how executives, managers, and employees convey emotional intelligence in the workplace.

In the candidate-driven market, this becomes especially important as companies will live and die by emotional intelligence. They will increasingly *need* to learn what makes their employees feel emotionally fulfilled at work on both an organizational and personal level—and implement policies, processes, and technologies that can help facilitate such experiences.

EIGHT SOLUTIONS FOR MANAGING A PASSIVE-AGGRESSIVE TEAM

Tracy Maylett

You've presented your plan to your team, and they appear to be on board. Getting everyone on the same page was, in your mind, the critical first step. Thankfully, they bought in.

When the time comes to implement the plan, everything falls apart. The team fails to follow through with their promises. Deadlines are missed, generally without much regret or accountability. You wonder whether they simply don't care or if they are intentionally sabotaging the effort. Either way, something's wrong. And this isn't the first time. In fact, rather than the exception, it's the norm.

The plan was clear, and you thought they were all aligned to deliver on the critical initiative. Except for one problem—your team's actions don't match what you all agreed to deliver, and they don't seem to care. In fact, they appear to be doing anything *but* what you agreed upon. You're working with a passive-aggressive team.

The Mayo Clinic identifies passive-aggressive behavior as "a pattern of indirectly expressing negative feelings instead of openly addressing them." When describing individual behavior, specific signs include:

- Resentment and opposition
- Procrastination or intentional mistakes
- Cynical or sullen attitudes
- Frequent complaints

Similar descriptions can be made of passive-aggressive teams. These teams:

- Actively or passively sabotage the efforts of others
- Procrastinate
- Deliver sub-par work or just enough to stay out of trouble

- Fail to acknowledge the urgency of priorities
- Disengage or lack commitment
- Complain or place blame, often covertly

A passive-aggressive team may appear to agree with an individual, request, plan, or important initiative. However, when the rubber meets the road, there is a clear disconnect between what is said and what is done. Passive-aggressive teams may range from behavior as mild as missing a few minor deadlines to delivering a product that meets only minimum specifications to blatant sabotage. Passive-aggressive teams are, at best, ineffective. At their worst, these teams can be severely damaging.

Dealing with a passive-aggressive team can be challenging. Unless handled directly, these behaviors seldom resolve themselves. Below are eight solutions for managing the passive-aggressive team.

1. *Look in the mirror.* Understand your role, as manager, in creating the behavior. We may mistakenly believe that individuals don't want to contribute. Sitcoms, movies, and comics are full of accounts of slothful employees trying to get by with as little work as possible. However, most of us aren't like that; we want to contribute. Assuming "they just don't care" is an easy cop-out. Understanding your role in

contributing to this negative behavior can be very enlightening.

2. *Make it safe*. When people don't feel safe, passive aggression may be the result. If they don't feel they can tell you what they're thinking, it's safer to hold back true thoughts and take it out in their actions—or inaction. And, if the team doesn't feel that you have their backs, they won't have yours.

3. *Give them a voice*. Often, passive aggression occurs because team members aren't heard. Not only does having a voice contribute to stronger commitment, it's often a major contributor to understanding what could go wrong—or right—with a plan. Team members who are closest to the work understand potential areas of success or failure. When these thoughts aren't voiced, not only does a manager miss out on a wealth of information, he or she is also far less likely to gain the commitment of the team.

4. *Explain the* why. Most managers have learned to communicate the "what"—they clearly outline what needs to be accomplished. Some are also good at outlining the "how"—steps needed to implement the plan. Few are equally adept at articulating the "why." When team members understand why the plan is

important, a manager can enlist the minds and hearts of the team rather than just hands.

5. *Communicate and align expectations.* Expectation gaps don't necessarily result in passive-aggressive behavior. But the outcome of unclear expectations is easily blamed on passive aggression. One of the most common reasons the plans aren't executed or changes aren't effective is because team members lack clarity around what's expected. Expectations, targets, and objectives weren't clearly aligned. It's hard to hit a target you didn't know existed. But this isn't just top-down. It works both ways. Managers must also be willing to hear and clarify team expectations.

6. *Proactively deal with negative behavior.* While these first five points were aimed directly at the boss, true passive aggression occurs at the individual and team levels. Refuse to tolerate damaging behavior. Point it out, and hold the team accountable. A manager who is not willing to clearly call out this negative behavior is simply reacting with another form of passivity. Create consequences, and hold the team to those expectations.

7. *Foster open communication and feedback.* It's difficult for a manager to know what's going

on if he or she isn't involved. Get in the trenches. Understand what's going on. Clear roadblocks. Then listen.

8. *Don't be part of the behavior.* Sometimes managers get sucked into the trap. Managers often mirror passive-aggressive behavior by falling into similar negative patterns shown by the team. Instead of being open with individuals, some managers take on the team's negative behavior, acting as if all is well while sulking, and waiting to ding team members on performance reviews or even terminating employees. Don't be guilty of the same negative behaviors of which you're accusing your passive-aggressive team.

Managing people with passive-aggressive behavior can be challenging, sometimes even more difficult than full-on aggressive behavior (at least you know where aggressive people stand). The key is to handle it both objectively and proactively, distancing yourself from the drama but also getting in front of it before it gets out of control.

BE SELF-AWARE, BE SELFLESS, AND THEN BE SELFISH

Ivan Misner, Ph.D.

Let's face it, networking is about you. Yet, that's the problem. Every day, millions of business seekers walk into networking events with one thing in mind: themselves. Don't feel guilty; it's totally natural. It's also counterproductive. While you shouldn't apologize for being a product of your baser (and selfish) instincts, you need to be aware of them when networking in search of new business.

So, are you destined to be a self-centered, one-way, "What's in It for Me" sponge? No! Here is some advice on how to manage it: Be Self-Aware, then Selfless, then Selfish.

Be Self-Aware

Never walk into an event or enter into a business relationship without knowing what you want from it. Does that sound cold and impersonal? It's not. It's smart because you need a plan. Although most people think this way, not all will. Admit it—this is something you need to know before leaving the office. You really need to think about and fully understand what your specific target market actually is. Does the person you're speaking to represent your target market or at least have the ability to connect you with those people?

Be Selfless

This is what our dear parents taught us growing up. Now that you've determined what it will take to grow your business, it's time to motivate your potential referral source to think of you when they hear of someone with a need for your products and services. The only way this will happen is if you absolutely lose yourself in your new friend.

Have you ever had a conversation with someone who hung on every word you said while making spectacular eye contact? Then every time you met them later, they did it again? This is the person you need to be for others.

Be Selfish

Some of you were probably getting a little anxious, but now you can relax and be a little selfish. Have you ever given a lot of business to someone and received nothing in return? Now, if it's your parent or a close personal friend, you can forgive that transgression. For all others, you've earned the right to have the favor returned.

So, if you know what you want from that relationship and you've made a lot of deposits into it, examine the reasons why they're not reciprocating. Perhaps you haven't taken the time to properly educate them. Do they understand what kind of referrals you'd like, of what quality, how many, and how you'd like to be introduced? You've earned the right but not given them the knowledge required to help you. You've not trained your referral partner— and that, my friend, is all your fault. So, arrange a time to meet with them and arm them with the information they need to start sending business your way.

There is a rhythm and a science to the relationship process. Ask yourself the question, "Does my business rely on referrals?" If the answer is "yes," then understand that referrals come from people. Referral marketing is unlike any other form of lead generation in that you are 100 percent reliant on other people to be successful.

So why put forth the effort? The answer lies in a survey conducted by the U.S. Chamber of Commerce a number of years ago. Nationwide, business owners responded that while only 2 percent of cold calls closed, 75 to 85 percent of referrals resulted in closed business. That makes them worth pursuing, worth having a system to go after them, and worth learning how to motivate people to give them to you. Cultivating referrals takes time, patience, and a commitment to the process. Are you willing to make that investment? Are you willing to be self-aware, be selfless, and then be selfish? Allow me to share a secret: the middle is definitely the hardest part!

HOW TO LEVERAGE EMOTIONAL DECISION MAKING IN MARKETING

Nathan Chan

When it comes to marketing, most brands are sneakier than you think. To be successful, a modern company can't just create a product that appeals to your pain points and offers a solution.

Instead, your favorite businesses create a connection with you on a deeper level. This is why you can sum up the advertisements and marketing schemes that prompt people to share and buy with a single word: *emotional*.

"But, surely we make decisions based on rational thought!" you'll protest. Um, no.

While many people think rational thought wins out, research conducted by the Advertising Research Foundation showed that people rely more on emotion than information to make purchasing decisions, with "likeability" being a top predictor of whether advertising actually coverted to sales. Human beings are emotional by nature, which means that many of our decisions—from what we eat to what we buy—are influenced by how we feel on any given day.

After all, if you think about it logically, your favorite pair of shoes is probably the same in structure as thousands of other pairs, but you rationalize that that favorite pair is better in some way.

The reason is that we're all emotionally compromised. The marketing efforts that companies make form a deeper connection with us and force us to fall in love with whatever they're selling. In fact, the most shared ads of 2015 were those which used emotional content.

If you're a marketer, this focus on emotion should be particularly important to you. After all, while it's important to educate your customers about your services and products, it's even more important to make them feel something.

So, if you're ready to get touchy-feely with your advertising efforts, it's time to start looking at the world of human decision-making and how you can use it in marketing.

Peering into the Emotional Brain

According to Antonio Damasio a professor of neuroscience at the University of Southern California, in a 2014 article, we need emotion to make basically any kind of choice. Through emotions, we connect brands and products experiences with our personal feelings and memories.

For example, if the first time you ate a burger from a local fast-food restaurant, you ended up being sick for several hours, you would probably associate that restaurant with disgust. It doesn't matter that you might have just had a one-off bad burger; your experience is still going to influence you in the long run.

In the same vein, if you associate going to that local fast-food restaurant with fun moments bonding with your family, then you'll likely go back time and time again—regardless of whether you really like the food or not. That's because our emotions create preferences which influence decision.

Damasio made his conclusions by studying people who had suffered damage to the emotional and rational parts of their brain. These people had no connection between those segments, and while they could process information, they weren't able to make decisions. Why? *Because they didn't know how they felt about the options they had.*

Delving a little further into the scientific part of marketing, a 2012 *Psychology Today* article has outlined some core areas where emotions interact to facilitate human choice. For instance:

- *Positive emotions such as happiness, delight, or satisfaction are more likely to build customer loyalty than anything else.* Simply put: If you can make your customer happy, that matters more than all the great guarantees and refund policies in the world.
- *Popularity is crucial.* Finding ways to make yourself more likable isn't a practice that stops after high school. In marketing, likability plays a huge part in brand perception and whether an advertisement makes a positive impact.
- *Emotional advertising can have a much larger impact on a customer's choice to purchase a product than the content within that ad.* In other words, it's the emotions you convey—not necessarily the product features—that sell your item.

- *Neuro-imagery shows that customers use their emotional brain rather than their logical brain to evaluate brands.*

Think about the last time you really enjoyed an advertisement. Chances are, you didn't like it because you just thought the information was intriguing but because it was funny, touching, smart, or interesting. We like advertisements for all the same reasons we like people.

Which Emotions Really Count?

There are plenty of core emotions. So, should you be appealing to all of them? Well, probably not . . .

According to a 2014 article from the Institute of Neuroscience and Psychology, the emotions that we use to make purchasing decisions use social constructs and interactions. They include:

- Happiness
- Sadness
- Surprise/Fear
- Anger/Disgust

While you probably assumed that "happiness" would be an emotion that all marketers should appeal to, the other options might surprise you. However, it's important to remember that negative feelings can be just as strong as positive feelings when it comes to provoking a reaction.

Making the Customer Happy

Happiness is simple and easy and a wonderful thing for many brands to embrace. After all, what company doesn't want to inspire a host of smiling, happy customers? Studies indicate that emotional articles and advertising that generate positive emotions are typically shared more often than articles that provoke negative emotions.

In fact, in 2015, the most shared ad of all time was "Friends Furever" by Android, which showed cute and inspirational friendships between animals.

Inspiring Sadness

Sadness creates a very unique type of advertisement. There's no point in a marketing scheme that makes your customer feel miserable and then suggests buying your product for no connected reason. Instead, you need to *use* sadness and then follow up with a product or service that can help to alleviate that feeling.

Studies have found that we are far more likely to empathize with sadness than any other emotion. That empathy can then be used to make us more generous and trusting. Sadness is best used when brands want their customers to emotionally connect and immediately develop that sense of trust and dependence.

Just take a look at this promotional video by MetLife Hong Kong showcasing the everyday struggles of a father.

Using Fear and Surprise

In all aspects of life, fear is a strong motivator. You push yourself to get out of bed and go to work because you're afraid of not having enough money to pay the bills. You make sure that you drive under the speed limit because you're afraid of hurting others or getting a ticket. Scaring someone into action is hugely effective.

You'll often find fear and surprise-based advertising in public service announcements for everything from drunk driving to smoking to global warming. This is because fear promotes change and tells us that we need to take action to protect ourselves and the people we care about.

Turning to Anger and Disgust

Anger is generally seen as a negative emotion. In marketing, most people want to avoid anger wherever possible, as the last thing you want is annoyed customers. However, anger is also a powerful motivator; it spurs us to do something about the way we feel.

Disgust and anger can force us to think about our perspectives or situations, and ask important questions, or speak up against injustice.

For example, an Emmy-award winning advertisement campaign "#Like a Girl" was created by Always to grab your attention by repeating a famous insult. The idea of the ad is to make you feel frustrated about a social stigma and compel you to become part of the change.

Speaking to Customer Emotions

In almost every aspect of marketing, there's a space available where you can insert some emotion or feeling into the mix. From the pictures of happy, smiling people on your website testimonial page to compelling videos that prompt your viewers to ask questions, there are plenty of tools out there that can help you to create emotional connections.

Some of the most effective emotional marketing solutions include:

- *Video*. An inspiring video can help viewers connect with characters on a screen and share their experiences.

- *Emotional copywriting.* Whether it's the words on your landing page that pack an emotional punch or the blogs that you write concerning important issues in your industry, words that really appeal to human emotion are sure to create a reaction.

- *Storytelling.* Human beings are naturally designed to love stories. Ever since your mother or father told you tales at bedtime when you were a child, you've learned to appreciate the simplicity and emotion of a story arc. In the same way, stories can shape the way we see the world through marketing, giving us an emotional investment in certain brands or companies.

- *Social proof.* Finally, the opinions of our peers are always going to have an impact. From those moments at school where you absolutely had to have a new jacket because all of your friends had it to deciding where to go for lunch based on five-star reviews: We use other people's opinions to form our own when we don't have any prior experience regarding a product or service.

Educating your customer is crucial, but it isn't enough if you want to make a lasting impression. Promoting an emotional response will help to create a long-standing relationship with any brand. After all, marketing strategies that don't make us feel anything are boring and forgettable—two things that you never want your brand to be.

ENTREPRENEUR VOICES SPOTLIGHT: INTERVIEW WITH DORIE CLARK

Marketing Strategy Consultant and Speaker

Dorie Clark knows a thing or two about emotional intelligence. At age 14, she entered Mary Baldwin College's Program for the Exceptionally Gifted, she graduated from Smith College at the age of 18, and she got her Masters from Harvard at the ripe old age of 20. Far from being just "book smart," Clark has worked as a journalist, documentary filmmaker, and jazz producer.

Described by *The New York Times* as an "expert at self-reinvention and helping others make changes in their lives," Clark is a marketing strategy consultant, professional speaker, and frequent contributor to Entrepreneur. She is the author of *Entrepreneurial You*, *Reinventing You*, and *Stand Out*. We caught up with her to discuss EQ and other topics.

Entrepreneur: In your work and research, how has the role of emotional intelligence, or EQ, come into play?

Clark: In many ways in the business world, there's "nothing new under the sun." Much great business advice is classic and timeless. So, how do you differentiate yourself in the marketplace and make people excited to work with you rather than a competitor? Often, that comes down to the personal connection you can cultivate with your audience, and that's frequently a function of EQ.

Entrepreneur: Your latest book is entitled *Stand Out*. That seems harder and harder these days with the glut of information on social media. What are some things emotionally intelligent entrepreneurs can do to separate themselves from the pack?

Clark: Through my research, I've discovered that there are three key elements to becoming a recognized expert. First, it's content creation: you have to share your ideas publicly so that others will know what they are and can start to seek you out. Second, it's social proof: you have to demonstrate credibility so people will be willing to devote the time to listen to your ideas. Finally, it's your network because you can't spread your message widely by yourself. If you cultivate these three elements, you can begin to ensure your ideas get heard.

Entrepreneur: You doubled your email list in one year. What's your secret?

Clark: During the launch of my book *Stand Out*, I did 160 podcast interviews in one year, and at the end of each of them, I promoted a lead magnet I had created, a 42-page self-assessment based on the book which they could obtain for free in exchange for their email address. People get way too many emails, so "subscribe to my email list" is not a compelling ask. But if you create a valuable resource that people want, they're often willing to subscribe and give your material a chance.

Entrepreneur: It's one thing to have people like your product/content, etc. But how do you get people to like you so much that they're loyal to you?

Clark: Loyalty is a function of trust and relationships built over time. Too many new entrepreneurs try to get the 'quick hit' and make a sale fast. Instead, it's about playing the long game. You have to share your ideas and content for a long time for free so that others will come to view you as a trusted resource. But when they do, you will have built a moat that is extremely hard for others to compete with.

Entrepreneur: Describe your technique of using "tiny bets to test ideas."

Clark: A key tenet of the *Lean Startup* methodology, with which I wholeheartedly agree, is creating a minimum viable product to test demand before you go 'all in' and spend a lot of money or time perfecting something. You first have to make sure you're actually creating something that people want! In my case, writing a blog post to see if people are interested in a concept before you write a book about that concept is a really good idea! I did this by accident with my book *Reinventing You*, which started as a blog post, but I now suggest this to other aspiring authors and entrepreneurs because it can quickly help you determine which ideas have traction.

PART II
PERCEIVING OTHERS—REFLECTIONS

Those who better perceive themselves, better perceive the actions and behaviors of others. This is a particularly useful and effective quality in business, where decisions are often based on feeling and instinct. EQ enables you to read the feelings of your customers and your co-workers so you can adjust the way you interact with them.

A happy customer is a loyal customer, and those with a strong or high EQ understand how to find ways to make their company more likable. That can mean creating marketing and advertising that appeals to their emotions.

A happy employee is also loyal and more likely to give their best effort. Emotionally intelligent leaders inherently understand this, providing a work environment that is respectful, collaborative, and positive.

Being highly perceptive doesn't come without a cost. You may be more aware of people's darker sides than those who walk around with their head in the clouds. Unfortunately, emotional manipulators and passive-aggressive types can make your life hell, but handled correctly and with sensitivity, you can manage even the most difficult situations.

FOUR WAYS TO OVERCOME GRIEF WITHOUT NEGLECTING YOUR BUSINESS

David Osborn

Everyone travels a rocky personal road—and business owners are no exception. Keeping your head in the game during a trying time is already difficult. Running a company while under emotional stress only compounds that stress.

This is something Dhiraj Rajaram is all too familiar with. The founder and chairman of Mu Sigma, Rajaram went through a divorce during which his wife sold her stake of the company, leaving Rajaram in total control of a multinational big-data delivery business.

It was a difficult time, but Rajaram and his team rallied, and the company has grown steadily every quarter since.

Even if your social life isn't tied to your business life, personal troubles can still significantly affect your leadership abilities. As Rajaram learned, balancing the demands of your business with a personal crisis isn't easy, but doing so successfully is vital to keeping your company moving forward.

Lightening a Load while Carrying a Burden

Balancing the various responsibilities of business and personal life is nothing new. In fact, according to a Bensinger, DuPont & Associates' study, 47 percent of people participating said that personal stressors affect their work performance. Many entrepreneurs may be specially equipped to deal with crises in business, but that same skill isn't always as effective when coupled with a personal plight.

At work, there's always more to do, and predicaments have definite answers. Work harder, make more calls, and put in an extra hour each day—these are all viable solutions to most business problems.

COPING AS AN ENTREPRENEUR

n a 2017 Harvard Commencement speech, Mark Zuckerberg told the story of turning down offers from some big companies during the first years of Facebook. "Nearly everyone wanted to sell," he said. "Relationships were so frayed that within a year or so every single person on the management team was gone." He describes this moment as his hardest while leading Facebook. "I felt alone. And worse, it was my fault. I wondered if I was just wrong, an imposter, a 22-year-old kid who had no idea how the world worked."

Doubt, loneliness, fear, stress—all of these emotions are familiar to entrepreneurs. While it is far easier to give into these feelings and give up, every successful entrepreneur has tales of how she persevered. It's no secret that Zuckerberg went on to become one of the wealthiest people in the world. So how do he and others survive the storms of uncertainty? A large part of the answer is that they rate high on the emotional intelligence scale. They can take care of themselves even when others couldn't care less about them.

Capacity enables us to manage setbacks and struggles healthily. While high EQers are not immune to hard times, they've developed robust immune systems that help them weather the storm. They also have the emotional maturity to recognize when they need help and the inner confidence to ask for it without feeling shame.

Like an athlete who trains their body for competition, the emotionally intelligent entrepreneur trains their mind for adversity. They recognize feelings of doubt about their endeavors as what they are—feelings that just reinforce how important their mission is. They recognize the power of being positive and grateful, even when your personal and professional lives seem to be falling apart all around you.

In this section of the book, you'll learn positive strategies for overcoming obstacles such as grief, loneliness, depression, and doubt. You'll see that you're not alone—even though it feels like that sometimes—and that emotional intelligence gives you the capacity to grow rather than wither away.

MANAGING YOUR MENTAL HEALTH AS AN ENTREPRENEUR

Kevin Xu

When people talk about entrepreneurship, most of the discussions revolve around the sense of fulfillment or satisfaction they get from building something out of nothing. While this may be true, there's another side to going into business for yourself: the price you pay.

That "price" is a psychological one. According to a 2015 survey, 30 percent of the entrepreneurs participating reported a lifetime history of depression. Another 29 percent said they were dealing with ADHD; 27 percent revealed feelings of anxiety.

Mental health issues, if not addressed, can have debilitating side effects—some of which may be detrimental to the business itself. Take anxiety, for example. When you're dealing with a choice, the anxiety involved may cause you to overestimate or underestimate the outcome of your selection.

Depression can have a similar effect on decision-making; it can lead to a more pessimistic point of view, one that renders you unable to use the information available to make the best decision.

What's more, feelings of apathy can lead to a lack of self-confidence, causing you to feel less valuable or validated by your work. Your employees don't just expect a salary from you; they want a reliable leader and exemplary role model to learn from and follow.

It's hard to give anything your all if you're not healthy—mentally and physically.

Taking Stock of Stress

Eighteen percent of employed respondents to the U.S. National Comorbidity Survey, a study of 15- to 54-year-old Americans, said they had felt some sort of symptom of a mental health disorder within a month of the survey. Although the signs that stress is affecting mental health vary from person to person, there are a few things to look out for—one of which is your temperament.

How do you react to unexpected news? If you're quick to be moody, become angered, or become irritated, there could be cause for concern.

The same is true for constructive criticism. You may normally be receptive to this type of input. But what if, of late, you've been unable to accept it, or you find yourself arguing over seemingly negative comments? That may be a sign you're under too much stress and it's now affecting your mental health.

You may also find yourself changing your mind with greater frequency or have an increasing level of difficulty making decisions—so much so that you start to neglect your responsibilities or drag your feet when faced with a choice.

Other signs can include a newfound paranoia about others around you (including trusted partners and investors), resistance to establishing relationships, and enough oversensitivity to others' opinions that it clouds your business and managerial decisions.

Shouldering the Load

Managing your workload is often the first order of business. But this is easier said than done for many entrepreneurs, and you might want to try the following to help:

1. Classify Your Workload

A 2016 CareerCast survey labeled unpredictability and deadlines as No. 1 and No. 3, respectively, on its list of the biggest contributors to work-related stress. Both issues can play a big part in an employees' daily capacity.

Your workload will generally fall into one of two categories: physically loaded or psychologically loaded. Make the latter a priority. The more psychologically loaded work you do, the stronger you'll get—no matter whether this work is successful or not. Increased amounts of this kind of work build a solid mental base and help you gain perspective on how to prioritize tasks during hectic or tenuous periods.

Steven Handmaker, chief marketing officer of independent insurance broker Assurance, noticed that his employees were struggling to manage their workloads and were bogged down with too many meetings, emails, and interruptions.

After Handmaker spoke with a consultant, he had his Assurance employees block out a certain number of hours each week for priority-work time. Employees subsequently reported being happier,

But, in your personal life, problems require the opposite: slowing down, listening, and being patient and selfless. Toeing both sides of the line can be extremely challenging. The burden weighs even more heavily when you feel as though you're on an island.

When my father was diagnosed with terminal lung cancer, I felt that I had no right to discuss it with my employees. They already had full-time responsibilities at work as well as their own personal struggles. You may be like I was: You don't want to expose your vulnerability. More importantly, it may seem unfair to place your personal burden on the shoulders of your leadership team and employees.

Still, I got through it, as did my company and my team. What I learned is that personal tragedy doesn't have to drag your business down, and maintaining your business doesn't preclude you from tackling life's problems. With the right team and the right game plan, this, too, shall pass—and you'll be better for it.

A Remedy to Rebound

Work-life balance is called that for a reason. When you're pulled too far in one direction, the other end of the spectrum suffers. For entrepreneurs, the stress of maintaining this balance can be exponentially worse, which is why many of them exhibit mental health issues and report feelings of depression.

If those numbers describe you, here are four tips to keep you on an even keel during a personal rough patch:

1. Keep the Door Ajar

A 2015 Interact/Harris Poll study stated that 91 percent of employees surveyed said a lack of good communication lessens an executive's effectiveness. You shouldn't burden or overload your team with the details of your situation, but be honest and acknowledge any personal challenge you're facing.

It's important that colleagues understand why their leader seems tense and stressed. This will quell rumors surrounding your demeanor or worries among employees about the future of the company.

2. Create a Support Net

Build and maintain a strong peer group of friends, family members, and loved ones outside work. If necessary, include a counselor, coach, or therapist who can help ensure you're not just burying your grief and avoiding it.

Take veteran entrepreneur Jeff Hyman, for example: He created the Startup Therapist to offer support specifically to startup entrepreneurs dealing with life's problems. A strong, supportive network of loved ones and peers helps you curb destructive behaviors and work through your grief.

3. Hand off Work

Virgin Group leader Richard Branson has called himself a big proponent of delegation. And that's a wise move: Handing off work to others is a good practice in general, but it's especially important when you need time to wade through rough waters.

Otherwise, you'll be forced to suppress your grief and carry on with "business as usual." So, be honest with your team to make delegating easier. When the right team members are in place, they'll be more than willing to pick up the slack while you tend to your personal affairs.

4. Return to the Surface

It's tempting to avoid the pain and circumstances of personal tragedy by burying yourself in your work—but don't. Ignoring a crisis doesn't make it go away, and you'll be more likely to experience a repeat, or something similar, in the future.

For example, if you ignore the true meaning behind a divorce, you may be doomed to experience another: Tamped-down emotional turmoil can manifest as chronic health issues later on.

Whatever your crisis is, be honest with your team about it. Delegate as much work as you can and lean on your out-of-work support system to overcome it. Otherwise, you may be forced to choose between keeping your business afloat and keeping your personal life in order. That's not a decision anyone should have to make.

FOUR TIPS FOR ENTREPRENEURIAL SURVIVAL DURING THE GRIEVING PROCESS

Dan Steiner

When your personal life seems to be falling apart, it can be difficult to focus no matter how many times friends and family members tell you to, "Get over it." But when you're running a business, you can't afford to indulge in the grieving process. People are counting on you to be present every day—regardless of what is going on after hours.

Relationship setbacks can be one of the biggest challenges an entrepreneur will face. Whether you're going through a divorce or the end of a long-term relationship, you'll likely be forced to deal with some heavy emotions. You may even start your day with the best intentions, only to find yourself staring blankly at your computer screen for long stretches of time.

When work demands are piling up and you don't seem to be making progress on healing, here are a few things you can do.

1. Set a Routine

One of the most devastating parts of a breakup is the disruption in your daily routine. Those daily routines you shared together are suddenly gone, replaced by silence. The first order of business is to find a new normal that includes the way you get ready for and come home from work each day.

You may also have to adjust the way you work. Instead of sitting down for eight to 10 hours straight, it may be better to do your work in short bursts, giving yourself emotional breaks. Use the Pomodoro Timer to force yourself to work in 25-minute increments before taking a break. During that break, give yourself permission to think about your personal problems in exchange for picking up your work again once the break is over.

2. Talk It Out

If people start telling you right away to "get over it," don't take this as an indication you shouldn't talk about it. A 2015 study found that reflecting on your breakup extensively in those early weeks can be much more healing than trying to shove it aside. Find trusted friends or family members who will help you talk it out. If this makes you uncomfortable, a licensed counselor can be a great resource even if you don't feel you need psychiatric help.

Often the mere act of talking out your problems to a counselor can be more healing than any advice they can provide. While talking about your issues, try to be productive, focusing on things you can learn about your relationship. It can be tempting to spend time wondering what your ex is doing, but this only hampers the healing process.

3. Change Your Scenery

If your breakup is recent, chances are you're sitting at the same desk you occupied when you were still a couple. Simply being in that space can remind you of how your life was just a few weeks ago. If possible, pack up your laptop and mobile devices and head for a new workspace. You could rent a vacation home for a couple of weeks, work from a friend's home or office, or rent co-working space.

You can return to your old space gradually as you feel better about things but in the meantime, you may find your productivity returns in new surroundings. Once your workday ends, find new hobbies and hangouts that will help you celebrate new beginnings.

4. Ask for Help

During the best times, entrepreneurs have far more work than they can handle on a daily basis. You may not be able to afford a full-time employee to help out, but part-time and freelance work can help you handle the overflow. A virtual assistant could help with responding to email, setting appointments, research, bookkeeping, putting together presentations, and many other daily tasks.

If the hourly rate is too expensive, a college or high school student may be able to help out after school and during school breaks. The hourly rate will be lower, and the students will have valuable experience for their resumes.

The end of a relationship is never easy, leading to weeks of grief and self-reflection. But for entrepreneurs, the mourning period can lead to lost productivity and angry clients. By finding ways to focus on work while still doing the necessary healing, entrepreneurs can recover more quickly and keep business moving forward.

THE FIVE BIGGEST PSYCHOLOGICAL HURDLES OF ENTREPRENEURSHIP

Jayson DeMers

As an entrepreneur, you'll face plenty of logistical hurdles. Quitting your day job, getting funding, finding a location, and hiring are just a few of the challenging obstacles you'll have to overcome.

The good news is that most of them are procedural, and though they may pose difficulties, they can be surmounted by following a logical process and committing yourself to seeing a final solution through.

The more difficult obstacles, however, meaning those most likely to impact your livelihood, are the psychological ones. The reason is that these are internal struggles.

Sometimes spurred by events and sometimes brought up spontaneously, these obstacles interfere with your ability to make decisions, the confidence you have in your own actions, your enjoyment of the work, and ultimately your capacity to continue as the head of your organization.

The following psychological hurdles are ones every entrepreneur must someday face, especially in the earliest stages of a startup's development:

1. Uncertainty

Uncertainty is around every corner, especially when you're first developing your business. You don't know if your market research is accurate. You don't know what competitors might emerge in the coming months. You don't know if your profitability model will work in real life as efficiently as it seems to on paper.

These uncertainties can get the better of you if you let them, but remember this: Uncertainty exists for everyone, and successful entrepreneurs are willing to embrace it because they realize that without risk, there can be no reward.

If this isn't enough to motivate you, understand that the worst-case scenario is never as bad as you imagine: Even if your first business fails, you'll always have a chance to build something new.

2. Instability

Beyond the uncertainty of your startup's infancy, be prepared for some inherent instability in your first several months. You'll have sudden surges of consumer interest followed by long droughts. You'll have random, necessary expenses crop up; major team members leave the company; and windfalls that will make all those losses seem insignificant.

To abuse a common cliché, startups are a roller coaster ride, but even if you enjoy that ride, the constant instability can get to you. People crave routines, foundations, and reliable structures. Without those, you'll experience much higher levels of stress, which can make you impatient, overly emotional, and miserable in general.

3. Responsibility

Being an entrepreneur means investing yourself in a venture in ways you've never experienced. Every decision you make, from naming the company to closing your first client contract, will affect your business' bottom line. As your business grows, this responsibility will grow.

And, eventually, it won't be just you on the hook but also your partners, employees, and investors. There's no easy way to overcome this other than by reducing decision fatigue in your daily life and understanding you can recover from a bad decision.

4. Balance

It's easy to get sucked into the daily work your startup involves, especially when you're passionate about the industry. It's your idea—your baby—and it's natural to want to invest as much time as you can into it.

Unfortunately, that desire sometimes leads to 100-hour weeks, long weekends, and sleepless nights, leaving you little room for anything else in life. What's most dangerous is that this imbalance often sets in without entrepreneurs ever realizing it. So, make sure to prioritize your health, and don't be afraid to take breaks.

5. Loneliness

Loneliness is a bigger problem in the entrepreneurial world than most people realize. Entrepreneurs are often depicted as naturally isolated geniuses who function contentedly as introverts when working on a project and then turn into extroverts when it comes time to talk to clients or the press.

In reality, though, every entrepreneur is pulling off a delicate balancing act, bottling up stresses, worries, and fears when he or she is around other people. This is a defense mechanism because telling clients or the press how scared you are could ruin you. Showing your anxieties to your team members could unsettle them and destabilize your company.

So, the only time you get to be your true self is when you're alone. This is a manageable lifestyle for a few weeks, but after a few months, it starts to interfere with your health. Instead, seek support—from friends, family, mentors, peers, and even counselors who are there to help you through difficult times.

Overcoming these hurdles isn't about ignoring them, pretending they don't matter, or avoiding them when they manifest. They'll stick with you, whether you like it or not.

What really makes the difference is how you respond to these hurdles. You can overcome them by accepting them, yet not allow them to interfere with your plans or your goals. You can ask for help from those around you. And you can make meaningful changes in your life to compensate for them.

All along, realize that your strongest asset against psychological turmoil is awareness. So, remain cognizant of these potential mental pitfalls, and keep moving forward.

DON'T LET THE LONELINESS OF ENTREPRENEURSHIP KILL YOU

Ray Hennessey

It's lonely at the top.

And that potentially could kill you.

We all know how stress walks hand-in-hand, knuckles white, with entrepreneurship because of the constant need to put out the fires in front of us. Entrepreneurs, after all, are crazy enough to believe fighting fires is more fun than fire prevention. We often look to stress management— exercise, more/less sleep, yoga/Pilates, Tequila

Avion—as a way to prolong our time in this madcap life we've chosen.

But we may be missing the real silent killer: loneliness.

We aren't talking about simply acting alone. It's important to remember how the theologian Paul Tillich viewed it, with loneliness expressing the pain of being alone rather than solitude, which expresses the glory of being alone. Many entrepreneurs start out believing (and, more importantly, trusting) themselves and themselves alone. After all, entrepreneurship generally comes from a product or idea sprung from your head, like Athena born from Zeus, and so a company is uniquely yours. It is a part of you.

Along the entrepreneurial journey, there are a good number of successes to share with your team, your stakeholders, and your customers. But there are a ton more failures and setbacks. Few people around you share in those.

That means you are essentially alone. You can only rely on yourself.

That is when solitude can turn into the more corrosive loneliness.

And that's where the health problems start.

A 2016 study from researchers at the University of North Carolina shows that loneliness can "vastly elevate" a person's risk of heart disease, stroke, and cancer, making it as dangerous to your health as a lack of physical inactivity in youth or diabetes in old age.

The research assessed loneliness across several life stages, but the overall picture is clear: loneliness can kill.

Advice is cheap, and readily ignored, particularly by the entrepreneurial set, but I'll try anyway. There are ways to avoid loneliness or at least take away some of its killing power. Here are just a few:

Collaborate

While your instinct might be to always go it alone, you run the risk of self-imposed isolation, which almost always leads to its close cousin, depression. Rather than isolate yourself, take on a partner or cofounder. For one thing, you'll have someone to talk with who is invested in your success. Second, it gives you the opportunity to get someone with complementary skills. Maybe you're a tech whiz, so you need someone who is a skilled marketer.

True, having a partner sometimes sucks, and you might find that even a founder needs to be fired down the line, but it can also be a wonderful, productive relationship.

Cowork

If you insist, in the very early days, on keeping all leadership functions to yourself, it might help to simply work adjacent to people just like you. Instead of operating your business from your kitchen table, spring on renting a desk or office at a coworking space. There, you can work alone amid a bunch of other companies doing the same thing. It's a great way to meet people who might be able to help you work out problems or network with like-minded founders to find funding or business opportunities. Plus, it forces you to put on clean clothes most days, which will also make you a far more desirable business partner.

Convert

Tillich's contrast between loneliness and solitude is instructive. Theologically, solitude is never really being alone since the feeling potentially brings you closer to your God. Practically, looking around you, seeing no one, and taking that as an opportunity for inner reflection, rather than outer isolation, can only be a positive for you. Call it prayer, meditation, or talking to yourself, reflection always gives your mind the pause it needs to recharge. Be still, and know you are not God but you can do great things.

Cry

I cry. I'm not ashamed of it. One Father's Day, shortly after my divorce, my kids picked up a set of grill tools for me for my new house. I bawled. Since then, my kids pretend to cry every time I pick up a spatula. We go through a range of emotions, but they really only get us in trouble if we let them manage us rather than the other way around. Loneliness is a feeling, nothing more. After all, you can be lonely in a crowd of friends. Like all feelings, they need to be felt and then addressed. Cry it out. Have that pity party for yourself. Then wipe your nose and move forward.

Get Help

Depression is the cancer of entrepreneurship, and more and more business leaders are handling their own mental issues more effectively. If loneliness is leading to a true mental illness, find a therapist. If you just need to talk about where your life or business is heading, hire a coach. If it's a spiritual crisis, find that bar where the priest and the rabbi always seem to walk in. Talk to your mentor. Call your dad. The greatest loss that comes from loneliness or depression is perspective. Only someone who isn't you can truly see you without the biases our internal mirrors show us. My experience has been that people generally want to help others, so unburdening is rarely a burden.

I'd never presume to tell people how to live their lives, and experience tells me that lonely entrepreneurs are the least likely to listen anyway. But life is too important to spend it lonely. Take a few steps to correct that, and I promise I'll leave you alone.

BELIEVING YOU'RE CAPABLE DEMANDS DOUBTING YOURSELF

Ray Hennessey

Believing in your potential to succeed is vital. You have to believe in your ability—believe you're capable—in order to win.

But you also need to believe you can fail, and you have to allow your actions to be governed by that.

Talking to entrepreneurs each day, I've found the biggest internal crisis comes from what they see as a lack of belief. When business suffers, customers don't materialize, or strategies fail, people often lose faith in themselves, question their mission, and give up. In short, they doubt.

Here's a secret: It's almost never a lack of faith that will sink you. It's a lack of doubt. More importantly, it's a lack of understanding of what faith and belief really are to the point where you don't honor your doubts enough to embrace them.

You need to have faith, and part of that faith is serving yourself a shovelful of doubt, of questioning almost every decision you make. In fact, the bigger a person's doubt, the stronger his or her belief.

Look at theology, which peddles in faith and doubt as its stock and trade. Thomas Merton, the great inspirational theologian, famously said, "Faith means doubt. Faith is not the suppression of doubt. It is the overcoming of doubt, and you overcome doubt by going through it. The man of faith who has never overcome doubt is not a man of faith."

Ponder that a moment. We tend to lionize the entrepreneurs who are singular in focus and purpose, who are so convinced of their mission that they pursue their business blind to the myriad consequences. We follow a narrative where we need to be so convinced of our path and our ideas that any doubt would derail the herculean effort it takes to succeed.

Yet, is it not better to give voice to our doubts, which, after all, stem from the same brain and heart that led us down this crazy, irrational, unsteady road we call entrepreneurship in the first place? The head and soul that convinced us to innovate, to try something new, to change minds, to help our communities and our customers also screams at us to go back to convention, to conform, to work quietly, meekly. Ignoring those screams often seems like the right thing to do for those of us who are ambitious and bold. But it's actually a wrong approach because we would be ignoring ourselves. And we alone know truly what's best for us.

Doubt can be a valued, constant companion, an emotional, nagging Sancho Panza we try to dismiss but know we could never live without. Doubt is our conscience. Doubt is our impulse to question all things, a reminder that scientific rigor holds more lessons than the meandering of our dreams. Doubt can be our enemy but also our champion.

Doubt is our check and our balance. Without doubt, we'd be foolish in our pursuits, rather than strategic. Yes, giving shrift to our doubts isn't easy. You might cry yourself to sleep, assuming you're not up all night obsessing over Quickbooks. Overcoming doubt means challenging yourself when it would be much simpler to let all the naysayers do that for you. It means flirting sometimes with depression and moodiness. It sometimes means more Hendrick's than tonic.

But all of that is worth it because, in the end, doubt will be your inspiration. Doubt will allow you to see your market more clearly. It will give clarity about business relationships, personal shortcomings, bad habits, and the hellish outcomes of your otherwise good intentions. Doubt can inspire you to change or, in entrepreneurspeak, to pivot. When you think of it, the Lean Startup movement is based on the appreciation of doubt. You put your idea out there for the world to see, get instant feedback, and make a decision of how to proceed. Sometimes you go forward. More often, you don't. It's a disrobing of your business before a room of customers with paper and charcoal in hand, ready to sketch their interpretation of your idea, your passion. One can't do that without confidence nor a willingness to be open to your internal doubts and those of others.

To be clear, doubting yourself doesn't mean giving in to the temptation of giving up. That's not healthy doubt but rather despondency and desolation. That can be just as destructive as blind faith. Rather, think of doubt as salt, which, in proper pinches, heightens all the flavors but, in excess, dries up our mouth and sends our blood pressure through the roof.

In the end, people don't profit from the belief in their infallibility. The flaw in that conceit is that you skip the infinite opportunities to learn. When you think you know everything, you miss the joy of discovery that our world offers us each day. For the weekend poets, that could be the gorgeous flowerets in the sunlight shining, blossoms flaunting in the eye of day. To the entrepreneur, it's more likely to be that customer you hadn't considered, that product you never pondered, or the partner you had never approached.

So embrace doubt, and let it strengthen your belief and faith in yourself. Rather than ignoring that voice in your head, honor your doubts enough to validate the belief you have in your own capabilities to shine.

HOW TO DEVELOP A POSITIVE RELATIONSHIP WITH FAILURE

Lena Requist

Entrepreneurs love few things more than their own ideas. These sparks of inspiration fuel the endless hours entrepreneurs devote to their businesses, and they compel investors to open their wallets in the hopes of making these ideas come to fruition. But even the greatest ideas can't overcome fundamental flaws.

In 2017 alone, many concept-fueled businesses have shut their doors. Beepi, a used car marketplace, was founded on a great idea but stumbled under bad prioritization. Quixey, a digital app assistant, folded as competition flooded the market. Yik Yak, an anonymous social network whose popularity was underscored by its young user base and a valuation nearing $400 million at its peak, shut down after cyberbullies ran rampant.

The failures of these well-funded companies sent ripples throughout the startup world. But failure itself isn't the problem—the inability to let go of a beloved idea is. Being an entrepreneur is all about having a healthy relationship with failure.

Failing to Fail

Many entrepreneurs are so fearful of ultimately failing to create a profitable and sustainable company that they overlook the smaller failures that litter the path to success. Failure can also be found in the lackluster marketing campaigns, ill-conceived software updates, and rushed hiring decisions that occur while trying to realize an idea.

I've fallen in love with a lot of ideas, but I eventually gave up or put on hold the ones whose weaknesses became so noticeable that even I couldn't deny them. For example, my company ONTRAPORT held Implementation Days to provide strategy, copy, and design services to support our clients in launching successful marketing campaigns. We knew small business owners would benefit from this additional insight on top of the capabilities our software tools offered.

This concierge service program met with some real success; we had a few deeply happy customers who were thrilled with the above-and-beyond efforts of our staff. A few cried while talking to our employees.

Meanwhile, we had thousands of people waiting. We had let the program veer off course while trying to serve individuals instead of our broader audience. I looked at the numbers and had a hard conversation with myself, concluding that although I loved the program, the business was suffering. These few happy people weren't covering our costs.

To deliver on our mission, I had to serve thousands, and that required putting Implementation Days on the chopping block. I now make a point to cancel programs at the end of each year if they don't make business sense or don't result in worthwhile ROI. Determining which ones make the cut, as well as how to rebound from such a loss, isn't easy, but a few steps can soften the blow.

1. Clarify Why an Idea Must be Abandoned

The financial devastation of throwing good money after bad can't be overstated. If an idea was once successful but is now struggling, its owner must attach a dollar amount to its current failure. To come up with the full cost, determine how much each stage of the process costs, how much it costs to pay your employees to do that work, and how costly it would be to replicate the process in the future.

Then, ask yourself, "If I have $1,000 to spend, what will truly get me closer to my goal?" You may determine that it's worthwhile to have your designers and writers implement marketing strategies for your customers because the results will outweigh the labor costs. Or you may, like me, come up with an alternative that still supports the goal. In our case, we decided to offer templates with guidance about copy and design strategy, allowing us to provide similar value to our customers but at scale.

2. Don't Abandon the Lessons Hidden in the Experience

Failure is hard, which is why most people don't want to go through it. Even watching other people fail is hard. My one-year-old nephew is on the verge of walking, but he keeps losing his balance and falling. But he'd never learn to walk if people kept grabbing him before gravity took hold. There's a payoff to his pain.

Likewise, if you're going to fail, you might as well make it worth your while. Write down the skills you obtained as a result of your failure. Get competitive with yourself: Compare the current version of yourself to last year's model. What are you now capable of doing differently to lead your company? What do you know now that makes you more valuable?

I did this at the end of 2015, a challenging year for my business. I found lots of problems, all of which were our own design. I could see exactly why we'd managed to find ourselves in the position we were in. However, we escaped layoffs and grew the company by three percent. Looking back, I realized that I hadn't prioritized data and analytics in my decision-making; I had failed to incorporate the right KPIs and how they were reported.

Today, everyone in the company receives a Daily Stats email first thing in the morning with what we call "cash the plane" KPIs. We then set up better weekly, monthly, and quarterly reporting for each of our teams during our weekly leadership meeting.

3. Develop a Grateful Mindset Toward Failure

The idea of thinking of failure with gratitude may feel like salt in the wound. But without the failures of 2015 that forced us to look at what we were doing, our company wouldn't have uncovered and resolved so many issues that would have prevented us from becoming the scalable business we are now.

I didn't just get comfortable with the list I'd made of the lessons I'd learned. I sat down with a colleague and put our lists together. There was overlap, but we'd each zoned in on different failures and overlooked others. That meant there was even more learning to be done. We adjusted our perspective and began embracing a new attitude: "How can we be open to that?" There's no longer a penalty attached to failure.

We also put our work in perspective. In our line of work, unlike that of doctors or firefighters, people's lives aren't in danger when we fail. Remembering that makes it easier to absorb the beauty of failure—it's part of the cost of learning, and it's why you'll be paid more down the line. Failing as an entrepreneur is a lot like surviving the grueling rigors of a difficult college program: You pay thousands of dollars, get no breaks, and endure lots of pressure. But the "Is it worth it?" question is answered at the end, when you wear that experience like a badge of honor.

Failure resembles grief: The only way out is through. And that makes sense because failure means grieving an idea that didn't pan out the way you'd hoped. But evaluating the data, embracing the lessons, and adjusting your attitude ensures that your failure will pay off with a much stronger company that can take a few blows and remain standing.

HOW TO BE GRATEFUL WHEN TIMES ARE TOUGH

Graham Young

"**B**eing grateful" is common advice that everyone has heard: We all know that focusing on what you have instead of what you don't have can make you a happier person.

But, let's face reality: It's difficult to be grateful when you don't feel that way. If things are not going well, the last thing you want to do is "look on the bright side" or "focus on the positive." You're entitled to feel skeptical about being grateful, right?

Well, not so fast because science shows that feeling grateful actually does make a radical difference. In his book *The Upward Spiral*, Alex Korb, a UCLA neuroscientist, says that focusing on what you are grateful for actually releases dopamine and serotonin into your body.

Dopamine is a neurotransmitter that helps control the brain's reward and pleasure centers. Serotonin is a neurotransmitter and is said to play a major part in mood regulation, anxiety, and happiness. When these two chemicals are plentiful, we feel good; when they are low, we just don't feel upbeat, plain and simple.

Korb also writes that the mere act of searching for something to be grateful for can make particular neurons in your brain more efficient, thus making it easier to feel grateful over time.

The Difficulty with Gratitude

A valid rebuttal to being tasked with feeling grateful is that it is hard to feel that way about things that come easy to us.

For instance, telling people to be thankful for the roof they have over their heads is hard for them to digest if they've never struggled with money. Or, telling someone to be thankful for the food they're eating may not work if they simply can't relate to someone starving in a distant land.

A related and common piece of advice is to list all the things you are grateful for and review it each day. While this is a step in the right direction, it's difficult for us humans to focus on so many different items at once. It's as if we're multi-tasking with our thoughts and feelings.

So, if you're trying to be thankful for the love of your spouse and the security of your job—at the same time—you may have a hard time getting a full sense of gratitude for either advantage.

Looking for ways to feel gratitude that make more sense? Here are ways to reprogram your brain to do just that:

1. Understand that Your Brain Can Rewire Itself

Neuropsychologists Rick Hanson, author of *Buddha's Brain*, and Joe Dispenza, author of *You Are the Placebo: Making Your Mind Matter*, echo the findings mentioned above. For the sake of brevity, they explain that our memories come from neural connections in our brain. When we focus on a particular thought or feeling related to that memory, those connections become stronger and easier for us to remember.

However, when we stop dwelling on those thoughts, the connections dissipate, making it difficult for us to remember why they bothered us in the first place.

So, although it may be difficult at first, you should continue focusing on things you are grateful for because that practice will get easier over time, as those new neural connections become stronger.

You will start noticing that those triggers that used to set you off don't anymore and that you're able to look on the bright or opportunistic side of things much more easily.

2. Make a List

The key is simplicity. When I am creating a performance program for my clients, I tell them to focus on how their three basic needs—safety, satisfaction, and connection—are being fulfilled.

When you are looking for what to be grateful for, focus only on one of these needs and pick only one thing you are grateful from among them. Don't overload your brain. Focusing on one thing at a time enables you to emotionally invest in it fully. Here are some ideas:

- *Safety.* What gives you comfort and security in your life? Think: health, your home, the city you live in, support of your family and friends, money, the freedom you have, a stable job, etc.

- *Satisfaction.* What activities are you able to pursue that make you feel good or accomplished? Think: realizing goals, hitting targets at work, engaging in hobbies you enjoy, exercising, reading a good book, driving your car, or enjoying the outdoors.

- *Connection.* What makes you feel closer, loved, and intimate or connected to others? Think: spending time with family and friends, meeting new people, volunteering, having a great meeting at work, enhancing a relationship with a colleague, or being part of a sports event or a party where people share the same interests.

If you are having trouble finding something to be grateful for, watch the news, and I'm sure you will get some ideas.

3. Focus on 'The Why'

After each item on your list, write why you are grateful for it. This will help you associate an emotional response with it and let it sink a little more into your brain. What impact does it have on your life? Why does it mean so much to you?

Gratitude is an emotion. So, to get its benefits, you must actually feel grateful for what you are focusing on. Just thinking about it or saying a list of things out loud won't do much.

4. Experience More

Don't worry if you are having trouble feeling grateful for things in your life. You're probably unaccustomed to this way of thinking. You just need to surround yourself with things that will make you appreciate what you have.

Unfortunately, we feel most grateful for things in life when we recognize how little others have. But if we elevate our gratitude while helping others, then we create a win-win. I suggest volunteering with youth or helping out families in need so you can see what they are going through and understand how much you truly do have.

5. Research

If you are still finding it hard to feel thankful, do some research and learn about the conditions other people are facing in the world. You'll have a different perspective on the issues you are dealing with. One strategy is to find a few videos that hit home and watch them every morning to remember how fortunate you are. This will kick your gratitude into action immediately with little effort.

The point is not to exploit the bad things other people are going through and use them for our advantage. It is to understand that the more we appreciate what we have in life, the happier we will be, the happier our kids will be, and the better a place this world will be.

ENTREPRENEUR VOICES SPOTLIGHT: INTERVIEW WITH SIR JOHN HARGRAVE

CEO of Media Shower

Sir John Hargrave used to suffer from addictions and crippling anxiety. Then he decided to do something about it. A computer geek, he approached his mental problems like he would a software glitch, reprogramming and debugging his brain for optimum results. He chronicles his discovery in his book, *Mind Hacking: How to Change Your Mind for Good in 21 Days*, which offers tips for how to take charge of your mind and banish negative thoughts.

Hargrave is now the CEO of Media Shower (www.mediashower.com), which connects blockchain companies with investors. He is also the publisher of Bitcoin Market Journal. He travels around the world speaking about his discoveries in the mind-hacking field. We asked Sir John (an American who changed his name through a court order) to share his insights into how to train your brain to be more emotionally intelligent.

Entrepreneur: Can our minds be hacked like a computer?

Hargrave: Yes, our minds can be "hacked," or cleverly reprogrammed, to develop any new habits of thought or action. As an example, I used to feel socially awkward with people. I'd be having a conversation with someone, but in the back of my mind, I'd be thinking, *Am I standing up straight? Do I have a piece of kale in my teeth?*

Once I became conscious of this behavior—which is the really difficult part—I was able to "debug" the problem back to its roots, which was this thought that I was bad with people. So I began reprogramming my mind with the positive thought loop: *I'm good with people.*

Then, whenever I was in a conversation or trying to meet someone at a networking event and noticing the old self-consciousness coming up, I would gently redirect my mind from the old program to the new one. By mentally repeating, *I'm good with people*, thousands of times, it turns out that now I am kind of good with people. So there's a wonderful self-fulfilling nature about mind hacking.

Entrepreneur: Can you hack your mind to have a higher EQ?

Hargrave: You could easily do the same reprogramming by using a positive mental loop like, *I have a high EQ*, or better yet, *I have a high IQ **and** EQ*. Neuroscientists now talk about "neuroplasticity," or the ability of the brain to form new neural pathways, at all stages of life. There's no limit to our minds, and our intelligence is not fixed at birth—it can always be growing.

Entrepreneur: What are some of the mind-hacking practices you recommend?

Hargrave: The hardest part is becoming aware of the buggy programming in our minds, the negative thought loops that hold us back: *I'm too old, I'm not smart enough, I will never find true love*. Our minds tell us these things, and we just believe them! "If my mind says it, it must be true." Someone once said, "No one has ever spoken as terribly to me as I do to myself."

We need to realize that *we are not our minds* and, in fact, we can become the master of our minds. The best practice for learning this is meditation. The basic meditation technique is simple: You sit quietly for twenty minutes, once or twice a day, eyes closed. You focus on the breath. When you notice your attention wandering, you gently bring your focus back to the breath. That's it.

Most people find this incredibly difficult, especially during the first few weeks. Your mind jumps around like a caffeinated monkey, and it seems like a waste of time. If you can stick with the daily practice for about six weeks, you'll start seeing real benefits.

And the benefits come not during meditation but in everyday life. Now when you find yourself getting angry about a co-worker or impatient about a traffic jam, you realize that it's *your mind* getting angry or impatient. When that happens—when you master your mind in daily life—that's a huge step forward.

From there, you can start debugging and reprogramming your mind using the techniques that I talk about in *Mind Hacking*. But it all starts with meditation because it's there that we develop the "strength training" to begin mastering our mind.

Another easy technique you can use right now is a game called, "What Was My Mind Just Thinking?" The idea is simply to ask yourself, as many times as possible, "What was my mind just thinking?" Keep count of the times you are able to ask the question and write down your final score at the end of the day. Most people find it really easy for the first hour, but then they forget about it! It's a simple technique that kind of turns mindfulness into a game.

PART III
COPING AS AN ENTREPRENEUR— REFLECTIONS

While entrepreneurship is often lauded for the freedom and satisfaction it affords, it can also take a toll on you psychologically. Entrepreneurs struggle with depression, doubt, loneliness, stress, and other challenging mental obstacles that, if not addressed, can lead to poor decision making and reduced physical health.

Those with solid EQ have the capacity to balance between taking care of business and taking care of themselves. They're able to take stock of stress before it takes hold of them. When they feel overloaded, they're masters at delegating. When they're faced with personal problems, they can be honest about it with themselves and others without letting it affect business.

Successful entrepreneurs don't run from self-doubt and fear; they add those emotions to their toolkits. Doubt propels them to have more faith in themselves, and they view fear (of failure or even of success) as something to get through, not run from. It takes emotional maturity to find light in even the darkest tunnels.

MAINTAINING YOUR EQ

magine that your best employee quits with no warning, taking customers with her, or you discover that your trusted CFO has been secretly stealing from you. These are nightmare scenarios for any business owner, but they're also par for the course. Every entrepreneur has their own personal horror story. It's how they handled these situations and the emotions surrounding them that separates great leaders from good ones.

It's one thing to learn how to manage a business, but it's quite another to learn how to manage your emotions when business gets rough. Those who are emotionally immature tend to react quickly to bad situations rather than step back from them and observe. They speak before listening, act before thinking, and judge before knowing.

Emotional management is a key component of EQ. It's the ability to handle professional and personal setbacks with maturity and wisdom. It allows us to have ownership over our emotions instead of the other way around.

Like any good manager, high EQers know how to motivate— even in the face of adversity or apathy. They know how to be likable and comforting but, at the same time, inspire respect and dedication. They understand the power of relationships, good communication skills, and teamwork. This all starts from within. You can't manage others effectively unless you know how to manage yourself.

The following chapters are a crash course in self-management. From dealing with criticism and rejection to building your emotional and mental fitness, these are the tools you need to become master of your own domain.

NINE PRACTICES FOR ACHIEVING EMOTIONAL MATURITY

Sherrie Campbell

Mental health is synonymous with maturity, and maturity is born of responsibility. You cannot be mentally or emotionally healthy if you are irresponsible. People with maturity understand a great truth; they understand that life is difficult. In being able to accept this fact about life, mature people learn to handle life in all of its difficulties, not expecting it to be different. They have learned to accept that not everything in life is going to be their way, show up in the way they thought it would, nor will the world change on its axis to make them happier. Mature people know for any change to happen it has to come from within themselves, and this is where success or failure develops. The only way to live a more fulfilling, successful, and purpose-driven life is when the choice is made to fully develop and live the attitudes and principles of a matured person. To follow is a list of those attitudes and principles.

Seekers of Self-Mastery

Mature people are passionate about self-development, psychology, and understanding the inner workings of themselves and the workings of the world. They are open to learn and apply the principles they gain from their explorations in personal development to all areas of their life. This type of growth mindset keeps mature people living more conscious and aware lives because they are able to live according to the life principles and wisdom gained both trough their own and the experiences of others.

Mature people typically have a team around them, from therapists to coaches, to keep them in check and on the path to living a life they love. Because they are supported, guided, and in the action of practicing the right attitudes and life principles, mature people more easily overcome the challenges that life inevitably brings them. Through self-mastery, mature people learn the art of turning life's lemons into lemonade.

Emotionally Intelligent

Life is going to be full of problems. The acceptance of this allows mature people to stay calm and think more clearly during life's more difficult moments. The whole process of meeting and solving problems is what gives life its deeper meaning. Mature people have established the emotional intelligence necessary to understand that life's difficulties are the cutting edge of what distinguishes one from being a success or a failure.

Problems call forth our courage and wisdom. It is only through being able to walk calmly and bravely through difficulties that the mature develop any sense of trust in God, life, or in themselves. It is through this process that they grow emotionally and mentally. As Benjamin Franklin says, "Those things that hurt, instruct." The emotionally mature learn not to dread but to welcome life's challenges for this very reason.

Positive Attitude

A positive attitude comes naturally to the mature person. They have faith in the concept that with enough hard work, patience, and persistence, things will work out. This type of attitude keeps mature people in a state of harmony with themselves and others because from their vantage point there is a way to make every situation a win-win experience. They have mastered the principles of being in mutually beneficial relationships and staying out of relationships that do not serve them or their ultimate goal.

Independent

Mature people have lived life and sought personal growth, which allows them the freedom of their independence. Through commitment and life experience, mature people have developed an independent mindset and live life following the principles and purposes they have set for themselves, regardless of what other people say and think. This sense of independence brings fearlessness to their personality and the resilience to be true to who they are. These are not people who follow the crowd or the establishment; they follow their hearts, passions, and desires.

Delay Gratification

Mature people have found a way to ground themselves in self-control. They know that those things worthy of their time will require their patience, persistence, and effort. Mature people are able to delay gratification. They enhance their experiences of pleasure by first dealing with and experiencing their pain and getting it over with. In other words, they place their responsibilities before leisure as the only successful way to live.

The mature are willing to tolerate feelings of discomfort long enough to find solutions to their problems. An immediate solution may represent gratification to many, but mature people know that the best solutions come with delaying the need to get rid of the problem quickly. The most lucrative solutions are found in the process of thinking through the problem.

Truthful

Mature people live with high integrity. They are committed to knowing, hearing, and working within the truth no matter how hurtful or stressful that truth may be. Mature people are also willing and committed to telling the truth even when it is humiliating and difficult for oneself or another.

They have an open mind to hearing counsel and to respond to reproof.

Responsible

Those with maturity live successful lives because they spend zero time blaming others for their problems. They take accountability for their actions as a way to further learn and grow. Life and life's circumstances, at the end of the day, have to be dealt with from our own will and volition, and admitting wrong is woven deeply into the fabric of mature people because they view humility and admitting wrong as steps up the mountain, not steps going backward. The mature person is able to understand that life is what they make it and that every person's destiny is within their choice. Those with maturity live life making conscious decisions knowing that whatever the result is, they are the one who is responsible.

Accessible

The emotionally mature understand the most important thing they can give relationships, projects, goals, or business is their time. When a person with maturity loves something and it is of value to them, they spend time with it, working on it, taking care of it, and enjoying it. They value themselves and, therefore, see their time as valuable and they have the deep desire to use their time well. For this reason, they will make themselves accessible whenever it is important. Because they value themselves and their own time, they also value the time they give and spend with others and make those commitments a priority in their lives.

Gracious and Giving

Mature people live with a natural feeling of thankfulness and appreciation for the expansive range of people, events, and circumstances in their lives. Because maturity is based in responsibility, mature people live with higher levels of happiness and lower levels of depression and stress. The emotionally mature turn their happiness into sharing and generosity. They offer helpful services to others as a way to spread their own wealth and joy in ways that circle back. When their giving circles back, the emotionally mature experience even deeper levels of pleasure, personal satisfaction, and gratitude for what they have been given in life to now gift back.

In short, maturity is a choice for everyone. The more you value who you are and what you have to offer, the more responsible you will be in taking care of yourself, your finances, your time, and your personal life. You can choose to live as a mature person. You can choose to live consciously with established principles and attitudes, or you can choose to live continuously beaten up and defeated by the struggles and miseries of life. Albert Ellis says it best, "The best years of your life are the ones in which you decide your problems are your own. You do not blame them on your mother, the ecology, or the president. You realize that you control your own destiny."

SEVEN THINGS MY GRANDPA TAUGHT MY BROTHER AND ME ABOUT ENTREPRENEURSHIP

Adam Toren

My brother, Matthew, and I can credit a lot of our success to our Grandpa Joe. After all, he's the one who introduced us to entrepreneurship in the first place; when we were just seven and eight years old, Grandpa Joe taught us how to sell Diper-Do stunt airplanes at a folk festival. He was a window through which we peered into the world of small business. Without his guidance, we may not have become the entrepreneurs we are today.

Sometimes intentionally and always by example, Grandpa Joe taught us many lessons we continue to use in each of our ventures. So you can have some of Grandpa Joe's entrepreneurial spirit and prowess, we're going to share seven lessons of his that stand out the most.

1. *Money doesn't grow on trees.* Money is one of the most important resources an entrepreneur can possess, and to say it should be used wisely is an understatement. Our Grandpa Joe taught us to budget well, give every dollar a job, and remain cognizant of how and where our money was spent. Cash doesn't just grow on trees; it's a result of hard work and patience, and for that reason, we've always managed capital with great care.

2. *Be slow to speak and quick to listen.* We have two ears and one mouth because we should listen twice as much as we speak. Be as great of a listener as you strive to be as a speaker, and in both instances, make sure you're on the same page as those with whom you're communicating. A truly great connection requires effort both ways. If you don't listen closely, you'll miss the valuable advice and inspiration coming your way.

3. *Understand that everyone wants to be understood.* Whether you agree with someone is inconsequential; *understanding* them is what makes or breaks a powerful connection. From day one of our entrepreneurial journey, Grandpa Joe taught us to be sincere with potential customers and clients and pay close attention to what matters to them most. This involves listening, sure—but it also involves validation. Even if you don't share one of your customer's values, legitimizing that value and supporting it will create a true connection. And a connection based on understanding is much stronger than one simply based on agreement.

4. *Keep your nose to the grindstone.* Laser focus and productivity are two goals all entrepreneurs share, but they're far easier said than done. Weed the distractions out of your life, surround yourself with people who motivate you, and constantly remind yourself of your goals (both short- and long-term). Leverage tools like planners, calendars, and smartphone apps to keep yourself organized. Share your intentions with others so they understand when you have to skip a night out. When you experience a bump in the road, shrug it off and regain

your focus. Keep your nose to the grindstone, and success will come.

5. *Be a good leader.* Don't confuse being a good leader with being a good boss. True leadership requires leading by example so your team can follow suit. It's your duty to stay on course despite distractions and unexpected obstacles, to delegate tasks to the most suitable people, and to reassess goals as needed. You should embody the culture you want your business to have. Managing a business requires you to be a boss; owning a business requires you to be a leader.

6. *Take calculated risks.* The very definition of entrepreneurship involves risk, but that doesn't mean you should make your decisions at the flip of a coin. Be attentive, do your research, and talk to people before delving into a venture with more than one possible outcome. Grandpa Joe taught us to surround ourselves with other entrepreneurs so their relentless ambition would bounce off of ours. Doing so only helped us as we built habits that would eventually breed success.

7. *Start 'em young.* Some people say it's never too late to become an entrepreneur, but Matthew and I say it's never too early. We

were incredibly lucky to have Grandpa Joe at our side during the start of our journey. In an effort to help today's kids experience young entrepreneurship the way we did, we wrote *Kidpreneurs: Young Entrepreneurs with Big Ideas*. It's the book we wished we'd had when we were kids. We also encourage young entrepreneurs to read and join online small business forums, where a world of information awaits. We think Grandpa Joe would be proud.

TEN WAYS TO MOTIVATE YOURSELF WHEN YOU'RE REALLY NOT FEELING IT

Barrett Wissman

Can you imagine Elon Musk ever waking up on a Monday morning only to press the snooze button repeatedly because he just didn't feel like going into the office? Or Richard Branson or Mark Zuckerberg?

It would be quite a surprise if you saw one of them laying on the sofa in a bathrobe trying to gather the strength to turn off the latest season of *Stranger Things* on Netflix and head to the office. Yet, many owners of small businesses have those moments. When that lack of self-motivation hits, some shake it off while others struggle to re-energize and press on.

That's when it's time to think about how you might work on a plan for topping up that self-motivation fuel when the tank starts to get dangerously close to empty. Here are ten steps to recharge your self-motivation levels:

Put More Meat on Those Goals

Perhaps your goals are lacking the muscle you need to truly energize yourself. If you haven't set more meaningful goals that give you something to be excited about and have stuck to the tried and true generic goals to increase revenue or add more customers, there's nothing there to sink your teeth into.

Let's go back to Elon Musk. He sets short-term goals that maintain his mental muscle of motivation, but he really flexes it with his longer term goals that fire him up. For example, he has the long-term goals of colonizing Mars, creating a hyperloop, and speeding Los Angeles traffic through underground tunnels. Until then, he focuses on converting Puerto Rico's power grid to renewable energy, adding solar tiles to houses across America, and adding to his fleet of electric cars to increase adoption. He's also working on those returnable rocket ships through SpaceX.

He keeps defining and feeding himself more creative goals to work toward. Keep your mind busy as a business owner and reach for those fantastic long-term goals while you use the short-term ones to fix the barriers to those longer range accomplishments.

Hang Out with Your Customers

Get out of your habitat because there is nothing motivational about sitting in an office whether it is a co-working space, your home, or an office building. There is nothing there that gives you a sense of purpose or rationale for what you are doing.

However, when you go to your customers and hang out with them, suddenly what you are doing becomes more visual, realistic, and just plain interesting. There is a dynamic quality to spending time with customers as well as hearing and experiencing what they go through.

You may have seen the show, "Undercover Boss," where a business owner experiences their business by working within it. Numerous CEOs have noted that it was insightful and gave them a completely different picture of their business, including customers and employees.

Of course, you don't have to hide. Go work and engage with your audience in person. You will feel reinvigorated and even come away from it with new ideas and overall renewed purpose for what you are doing. Plus, your customers will be pleased to see you care that much to hang out with them, which impacts their experience.

Set a Personal Mission

Every business should have a mission or vision statement. This is simply something that describes the broader goals, culture, and underlying core values of the business. While you may already have that, it is not going to necessarily motivate you to keep going. Although it is something that shows why you are in business, it does not really cover your own purpose.

Creating a personal mission statement is motivational because it states why you are doing the business and what you want to achieve from it in relation to your own professional and personal development. Paste it onto your calendar app so that it pops up each day and use it in your social media status updates to remind you and others about your philosophy, which goes well beyond just your business.

Take Time for Yourself

Running your own business can completely consume you. Once you are in it and handling daily operations, putting out those "fires," and wearing all those hats, you lose track of time. Days melt into weeks and then months before you realize you haven't taken a day off. With all that work and no play, Jack or Jill becomes a dull boy or girl. No one can keep going at full steam all the time.

While we may not be able to have our own personal Necker Island like Richard Branson to escape to, there are ways to actively stop the work-work cycle and live a little. Schedule time off each day to decompress and do something you like. This could be a hobby or time with your family. Don't compromise those special moments because you will find yourself becoming more resentful of your business, and your motivation will suffer.

There are some business owners who have even gone on sabbatical, letting a trusted team member run their business for a few weeks, a month, or even longer. All say they return with greater enthusiasm and the motivation to take their company to the next level.

Savor Success

So much is said about continuing to look forward. However, to stay motivated, it's a great strategy to look back on where you have come from on this journey to build your empire. Reflect on those little and big wins that occurred along the way.

It's like looking back on your school yearbook or old photo albums to see how much your life has changed. The same can be done for your business. You'll remember the challenges and how you felt at those moments. Those reflections often lead the mind to wonder about what your life (or business) will look like after a few more years when you do this same revisit of the past.

This is the time to take those press mentions and compile them on your website and social media pages. Actively reliving these past successes will tell you what you have achieved while the act of sharing those with others and their reactions will fire up the self-motivation.

Mentor Others

Nothing can motivate you as much as helping others. Not only does it more effectively frame your reality when you see others experiencing similar challenges or business decisions, but it also inspires you to go back and change things after working on other startups. Plus, it just feels good to help others and know that you have made a difference for them, perhaps even serving as the stimulant for them to boost their own motivation.

Sign up for mentoring sites or businesses that look for experts like yourself who are willing to volunteer their time to help other founders and owners. There may also be those within your own network that are asking questions in online forums where you can lend your knowledge and expertise.

Set—Then Change—a Routine

A routine helps with discipline and keeps you on course with productivity and balance. For example, leverage "John Meyer's 8 for the Day" routine. However, over time, it can have the opposite effect and bore you to death, causing you to become unmotivated.

Use the routine as your foundation, but then consider changing up that routine every other week or month. It depends on your personality as everyone has a different place where they hit a wall of monotony. That means you will need to create different routines that you can rotate in or out to keep your time as interesting and stimulating as possible while staying on target with what you want to accomplish.

Immerse Yourself in Inspiration

There is a lot to be said for content out there in terms of its ability to inspire to keep working toward greatness. From TED talks and podcasts to blogs from your fellow entrepreneurs, regularly take a moment to check in with what others are thinking about and sharing based on their own experiences. The emotional connection you make with this content can spur you onwards and upwards.

Search for YouTube channels, blogs, podcasts, and articles on motivation and then subscribe to them so they arrive in your inbox. Go see speakers who cover a wide range of topics that impact your business and participate in events, networking socials, and conferences for further inspiration.

Contribute to Your Community

You may not realize how much your small business is already positively impacting the community. There were 28.8 million small businesses in 2016 that accounted for 99.7 percent of U.S. businesses! As David M. Kirby wrote in the *Huffington Post*, "small businesses are vital to the future of the United States." Your business is boosting the local economy.

From there, it's time to move from think to act. Give back to your community through donations and volunteer work. Bring in passionate interns from local universities to work for a semester. Getting involved with your community can mean further interactions with customers. Even if they are not your target audience, it puts your life and work in perspective when you go help others in need.

Don't Go Solo

The life of a business owner is lonely at times, especially when you are a one-man band, work from home, or use a virtual team. Don't spend all your time alone because it is difficult to stay motivated.

Instead, build a support network that will help and encourage you whenever you need advice, inspiration, or just want to vent. This could be a mentor, your spouse, best friend, or fellow small business owner.

Also, working alone tends to prevent you from doing some of the other things on the list because you have no remaining time to do things after covering all the roles and responsibilities in your business. If you have the resources, hire freelancers to cover many of those tasks so you can use the other tips here plus spend more time on the higher level aspects of your business that most likely hold all the excitement.

Losing your "mojo" is normal and happens to every business at some point. Don't focus on it or let it stress you out. Take action through this list of tips, and you'll find that your self-motivation returns and even grows.

SEVEN EMOTIONAL MANAGEMENT PRACTICES THAT PROPEL SUCCESS

Sherrie Campbell

Poor emotional management can destroy a person's personal and professional life. A person in business who doesn't possess a well-kept check on his or her emotions is seldom well-liked or respected. Being a professional requires maturity, dignity, and integrity. We cannot respect those who cannot control themselves emotionally in life or in business.

If we have poor emotional management skills our egos and pride trump our intelligence and knowledge every time. How we manage ourselves emotionally is of even greater importance in the business world than our skill or talent.

Observation

To manage our emotions well we must develop the ability to act as the observer of our own emotional experience without getting caught up in assigning any judgment to what we're feeling. Hard to do? Yes. It's hard to do because our minds want to judge the goodness or badness of our situation immediately in an effort to come up with strategies to help us through our situation. When we're emotional, however, we are batting less than average on what the objective truth of our situation is. When we allow our judgments to define our experience without much thought or consideration, we end up reacting rather than responding, causing us to act out emotionally rather than rationally.

We must learn to observe and understand the emotions we are experiencing without the pressure to do anything with them or about them. We must discipline ourselves to sit with the discomfort and take an active curiosity in analyzing what we feel without any need to define it, deny it, or change it.

This helps us balance. There is no need to instantly reject situations or emotions just because they are unpleasant. Not everything that feels unpleasant is bad. If we can remain objective, we can turn what feels uncomfortable into something productive.

Acceptance

When we feel overwhelmed with emotion, we become instantly adrenalized for survival, making it extremely challenging to experience our emotions as separate from our intense and automatic impulse to act. We may not be able to choose what we feel, but we can come to recognize when we are reacting and be proactive about it.

Take a step back. It is amazing what taking a moment can do to settle an unsettled mind. It helps us to be less judgmental of ourselves and our situation, stalling our reactive impulses to speak or act before thinking. When we can hold on to ourselves and sit with what feels uncomfortable, it helps us to accept what is happening. Acceptance helps us tolerate chaotic emotions with a greater sense of composure, less fear, and less resistance.

Impartial Openness

When we judge what we feel as right or wrong, our emotions have ownership over us, giving us the feeling that we have zero agency over handling them. Whenever we react from a black-and-white sense of right or wrong, we come off as self-righteous. We force our opinions onto others and the situation in a fixed and unfair way. Black-and-white thinking is incredibly limiting to other options that could generate solutions with a much more effective result.

When we choose in our choice to be open and impartial amidst our challenge, it helps us take in the bigger picture, including the ideas and emotions of others. This allows for situations to be approached in a more fluid and creative manner, rather than from selfishness and our own best interest. Being impartial garners a greater wealth of potential directions to be analyzed and used, rather than reacting from a fixed and fearful position the ego has decided is best.

Non-labeling Awareness

When we force ourselves to stay directed towards being an active participant in controlling our emotions, we are less likely to get caught up in old ideas or memories that have no real relevance to what is currently happening. We don't need to label anything that is happening right now as good or bad. We must train ourselves to look at what is going on through the lens of, "Right now this situation is what it is." What is bad right now is fluid, so be patient and stay in a place of not needing to label a situation too soon. There is great value in letting things unfold naturally.

As hard as it is not to have an agenda or to try and exert some sort of control over our situation, allow the discomfort to untangle itself. We must work to stay out of rigid patterns of thinking and behaving. In doing this we remain open to resolutions that will naturally surface. When we choose not to label, we see things from a higher level we never could have reached had we pigeon-holed, judged, or reacted.

Constant Presence

When we are emotionally activated, we tend to swing widely into our past and to project failure or success onto the future, which takes us completely away from what is going on right now. Whatever is happening right now, let it marinate without reacting impulsively. We not only have to manage our more negative emotions, but we also have to manage our heightened positive emotions to make decisions based in reality rather than on the fantasy of the future or the horrors of the past.

Stay connected to what is happening now. Hold onto yourself, write down or contemplate options of decision making, have discussions about what is happening with others, and then, when things are operating from an emotional balance, move forward with a decision. In forcing ourselves to stay present, we stop ourselves from operating on "automatic pilot," which keeps us locked into the mental dream of the past or the future. New, fresh, and innovative ideas come from being able to slow down and think rationally about what is unique to our current situation.

Empathic Awareness

All of the emotional reactions we have in life or business are learned. Through experience, we have learned which people have been hurtful or harmful and which people have been honorable, kind, and respectful based upon how they treated us. Empathy means letting go of the drama of being stuck in our own self-centered viewpoint in an effort to make more sound decisions.

Being empathic involves taking a completely different observational stance of our own reality and our experience of it. It involves letting go of the drama of Self—of me, my, mine, and I. When we come from selfishness, we see everyone and everything as our opponent. Empathy allows us to see others as teammates. When we are self-centered, we tend to make irrational and selfish decisions. With empathy, we have a team of others to help us make rational and successful decisions.

Everything in life and business is fluid. Things may temporarily get stuck, but it can't stay in a stuck state forever. It is important, when emotional, to activate our minds in ways that involve our abilities to observe the natural changes occurring in the present moment. The less distracted we are by our internal experience, the more calm, patient, and curious we become to the natural changes which inevitably take place in any business. This allows us to work smarter rather than harder. When we panic, we suffer and overcompensate. Everything is temporary, so this means we have time to slow things down and think things through before acting.

29

TEN WAYS TO BECOME A SUPER-LIKABLE PERSON

Deep Patel

Do you make people feel comfortable and welcome when they are around you? Do people feel appreciated, understood, and accepted by you?

Likeable people know how to endear themselves to others from the get-go. They understand the importance of presenting themselves as being genuine and willing to connect. Do this, and people will see you as someone they want to have a conversation with and hang out with.

It may seem like charismatic people are born charming, but the truth is that likability can be learned and honed just like any other skill. Start with these ten secrets to become one of those friendly and super-likable people that everyone feels comfortable around and wants to get to know better.

1. Have a Friendly, Open Demeanor

The fastest way to kill your likability is to come off as fake, aloof, or indifferent. Chances are you don't mean to be seen as negative or disinterested; you may just feel uncomfortable in some social settings or are naturally more reserved.

But keep in mind that others are trying to get a read on you. When you present yourself as closed-off or snobby—even if it's unintentional—nobody is going to be excited about getting to know you. Let your guard down, and don't be afraid to be yourself.

Be aware of how you are presenting yourself to others and do your best to develop an open, friendly demeanor. Let your personality shine through and practice opening up, in both verbal and nonverbal ways. Smile. Make eye contact.

Nod to show you are listening. Lean in when someone is speaking to you. People are naturally drawn to others who are genuine and who are comfortable in their own skins. So be authentically *you*—and remember, it's often not about what you say verbally but what your body language is saying.

2. Listen First, then Speak

So often, we are in a rush to get a word in edgewise when we are talking to others. When someone else is speaking, we only half listen while we are contemplating how to respond. By being too quick to insert ourselves into a conversation, we often miss a chance to establish a connection with the other person.

If you cut into a conversation, you can make the other person feel like you are shutting them down before they have a chance to fully explain.

Act as if the person you are speaking with is the most important person in the world. Practice actively listening to them—really concentrate on what they are saying. Don't jump in to offer advice or try to solve a problem. But do ask follow-up questions. This will help them feel heard and let them know that you sincerely took the time to understand what they were saying.

3. Don't Hog the Spotlight

We all love to take the spotlight from time to time. If you're extroverted, you may live to be the life of the party. But people who are consumed with getting attention may be missing all kinds of opportunities to offer value and be of service to those around them. If you come off as conceited or self-important, people may not want to spend a lot of time around you.

Likable people don't want to hog the spotlight; they want to share center stage. They seek to shift the focus to those around them. They know how to praise others without being excessive.

They understand the importance of bringing others into the conversation and pulling a quieter person out of their shell. The bottom line: stop pining for people's attention and look for ways to include others in the conversation.

4. Ditch Your Devices and Focus on Who's in Front of You

Put down your smartphone, step away from your digital devices, and focus on the humans in front of you. Instead of scrolling social media, just socialize. Mingle with people in real time. If you are attempting to monitor your email or return text messages, you will fail miserably at building a relationship with the live person you're ignoring.

When talking with another person, fully commit to that conversation and focus your attention on them. Technology has its time and place, but too often, we make it the focal point of our lives. Go old school and spend some time making small talk with those around you to begin building real relationships.

5. Synchronize Yourself to Those Around You

We may not realize it, but when it comes to social interactions, we all like a copycat. We naturally synchronize ourselves to those around us. When someone smiles, we are inclined to smile back. This begins in infancy: babies naturally imitate the facial expressions of those around them.

This social synchronization is an important way of building rapport with others. It means we subtly imitate the gestures of the person we are talking with. We may unconsciously mimic their breathing and body posture as well. Matching your voice and tone to the other person is a powerful tool for building a feeling of affinity and connection.

The other person will automatically feel like you are on the same wavelength with them and empathize with them. So when you have a conversation with someone, be aware of how you are mimicking them and try to discreetly match their body language and behavior.

6. Ask Conversation Starters

Knowing how to start a conversation on the right foot is key to immediately instilling a sense of belonging and connection. Questions get the other person talking and engaged in a conversation, but the trick is knowing what questions to ask.

An open-ended question invites the other person to offer their opinion or give their thoughts on a subject. The idea is to use questions that get a conversation going. Some examples include: "What was the last funny video you saw?" or "Who is your favorite musician/actor/comedian?" Think of questions that begin with who, what, where, when, why, and how.

On the other hand, a closed-ended question is one that can usually be answered with a yes or no response. For instance, asking, "Are you feeling better today?" is closed-ended, and the person doesn't have to answer with anything more than yes or no. Asking something like, "How are you feeling today?" invites the other person to share something about themselves.

7. Be Open-Minded

Likable people are seen as approachable and personable because they are open-minded and willing to talk to and listen to many different types of people. They avoid having preconceived notions or passing judgment on others but are willing to hear others out and get different points of view.

Of course you will meet people you disagree with, but the idea is to allow others to have their say so you can better understand them and make them feel heard.

Allow others to offer their thoughts and ideas, and then respond by sharing your own beliefs and feelings—always in a considerate and respectful way. Do this, and you will promote deeper discourse and discussion.

8. Be Reliable and Balanced

Being moody, short-tempered, or gloomy are the opposite of likable. People who are known for their unpredictable and fluctuating moods aren't making anyone's "most lovable" list. In fact, people will actively avoid you. If you want others to be comfortable approaching you, people need to feel confident that you are even-tempered and reliable.

You can have a bad day or be in a sour mood sometimes, but when you are, remember this little gem: you don't have to express every thought or feeling that comes into your head. Sometimes it really is better to nod, smile, and say nothing.

Be honest when you are stressed or frazzled— give yourself a little extra space. Don't let a bad mood control you. Instead, treat each new person you come across as a fresh start and don't let previous entanglements influence how you handle someone.

9. Look for Shared Interests

When it comes to establishing a rapport with someone, look for ways to establish common ground through shared hobbies or interests. This is when having a variety of interests and a diverse background will come in handy. It may help to do a little homework ahead of time if you know you will be meeting new people.

Do you both enjoy certain activities, watch the same television shows, or enjoy reading similar types of books? Perhaps you know people in common, are involved in similar community organizations, or have done business with the same company.

There are many ways that you may overlap with someone. And if you don't have something in common, chances are they have a skill or hobby that you are interested in and would like to learn about. View each person you meet as an opportunity to learn something new.

10. Say What You Mean Verbally and Nonverbally

We've all had the experience of asking someone how they are doing and they say they are fine but their body language indicates something else entirely. They may avoid eye contact and have a scowl on their face while tapping their foot and using an angry tone of voice. The fact is, we don't believe a person who uses mixed signals like this. We find it confusing. It inhibits our ability to build trust with them.

One of the most powerful ways to begin a conversation is to face the person directly. Look the other person in the eye and avoid bad body language—no crossed arms or slumped posture.

Make sure your facial expression is open and agreeable and you are using a pleasant and composed tone of voice. If you do this, you are telling the other person you are enthusiastic about communicating with them.

One of the most important elements in likability is to make sure that all the nonverbal messages you send the other person are congruent with the actual words that come out of your mouth. Say what you mean verbally and nonverbally, and others will feel closer to you and more confident in trusting you.

Being likable is not the same as being nice. When we try to please everybody, we often end up pleasing nobody. Likability is different. It's a quality that you can learn and practice that makes others want to be around you, listen to you, and trust you.

30

FIVE WAYS CRITICISM AND REJECTION BUILDS YOUR CAPACITY TO SUCCEED

Sherrie Campbell

No matter who you are, when you have a dream and are committed to achieving it you will face critics and experience many rejections. You will face people who have the outright desire to take you from your path. Many people, who may be in power, will use their position to push down ideas that are not in line with their own, or ideas they do not understand or value. Just as detrimental are the "caring concerned" who, in trying to protect you from your unrealistic dreams, keep you from them.

The greatest obstacle to success is your fear and belief in what a critic says. Instead of running or quitting, make the emotionally strong choice to move forward, in spite of perceived setbacks, understanding that sometimes it is only *your* opinion that matters. In that way, you will receive five powerful gifts from the people and situations that don't wish you well at all.

Emotional Strength

The pursuit of success nearly guarantees the more you seek to fulfill your purpose, the more obstacles you will face. As you come across naysayers, you must learn to not integrate their fears into your own belief system and decision making.

Pursuing a dream is emotional strength training. The more motivated you are to make a difference and change the world, the more you rise in your success. The more you want to create and lead, the more rejection and criticism will show up on your path in an effort to derail you.

This is an opportunity to develop the skills, strategies, and resolve to continue forward. In this way, your naysayers become your greatest motivators. They fuel your desire to show them just how wrong they are about who you are and where you are going.

When in doubt, remind yourself that naysayers belittle others in an effort to stop feeling so little themselves.

Self-Control

Receiving criticism and rejection is common when your pursuit is doing important things in the world. Force yourself to become conscious of the rude, ill-informed, and unkind people who emerge to tarnish your shine. With an awareness of them you gain more control over your emotional reactions to them.

Negative people lurk around every corner. The reality is that things aren't going to be fair on your way to the top. Accept that. Because you will interact with a fair number of these people, you have the opportunity to develop unbeatable self-control.

Critics love to get under your skin and push you off balance. It gives them a sense of power. Therefore, use these people and experiences as exposure therapy until, eventually, rejection and criticism have little to no power over you. By weathering exposure to the negativity of others you develop control of your emotional reactions to their efforts to set you back.

Ability to Refocus

Learn to say "next" to every "no." Rejection is not the end of the world, nor does your idea merit being discarded. Look for gifts in the feedback that comes with rejection. Accept what can be successfully applied to refine and make your idea better. Then, move on.

Each rejection leads you closer to that "yes" you are seeking. Each "no" feels like another step back but is really bringing you one step closer to realization of your dream.

Refocused energy is the most creative energy. You have the opportunity to refine, repurpose, and perfect what is already in place. Rejection, if you allow it, can fuel your deep desire to succeed. To be successful, you must compete, compete, compete.

Fearlessness

Success is all about risk. Each time you put yourself and your idea out into the world you risk rejection and criticism, so do not be shocked or dismayed when it happens. Success *is* about getting knocked down, learning resilience, getting back up and risking again.

Each time you take a risk, you become emotionally stronger. Each loss provides the information your pursuit needs to determine what new direction to take. Risk takes courage and courage can only be developed by doing courageous things. Giving up takes zero effort; getting up takes resilience.

Most of the happiness derived from success is not monetary but comes from the confidence you build along the way as you risk, fall, try again, risk, and then succeed.

Unwavering Belief in Your Purpose

When you believe deeply in what you are doing, what you are creating, and what your ideas stand for, you develop the resilience to withstand all rejection and criticism. There is nothing more profoundly necessary for true success then a deep and unwavering belief in your purpose.

There will be all kinds of people who want to shrink your ideas or steal them. Others will want to use you for your idea or simply tell you your idea is worth nothing. Pay attention to who you listen to. Be smart about who you choose to pitch your ideas to. Pay attention to your gut instincts. Protect your ideas and only share them with those whom you respect. Do your research, and work with like-minded innovators.

With deep belief, you can remain hard working and quiet because your success will do the talking.

Determination

What kind of true success can really come without real effort, real labor, real heartache, and real sweat? Success does not come to the weak. No journey is devoid of self-doubt or setbacks. Success is a matter of standing up to your challenge. It is a matter of commitment and not giving up. It is about getting up and suiting up, even when things look bleak. It is having the complete resolve to pursue your higher purpose.

There is nothing unrealistic about a dream that is in complete alignment with your purpose. If what you are doing ignites your passion and inspires you to plan and persevere, then you will, without a doubt, achieve what you have set out to achieve. Any person with a deep conviction and commitment will succeed. Therefore, the only opinion about your dream that really counts is yours. The negative commentary of others merely reflects their limitations, not yours.

Success is built upon your own determination, not managed by anyone else's opinion. This is why success is never a straight shot to the top. None of us would be nearly as successful as we are without the gifts of the naysayers, the tough rejections, or the harsh criticisms. It all depends upon what you choose do with it. To be a standout success, you must learn to control your emotional reactions and turn all of the criticisms and rejections to serve as your greatest advantage. Most importantly, see the value in it all, and be thankful all along the way.

Success, at the end of the day, is your greatest revenge. Be sure you are the last one standing.

THREE POWERFUL TIPS TO IMPROVE YOUR EMOTIONAL AND MENTAL FITNESS

Julian Hayes II

Let's face it, as entrepreneurs we're busy trying to make our impact in the world while also keeping our personal world in order. Running your own business requires a lot of work. And more often than not, we let business and work take priority over health.

But without your health, you're only going to be a shell of who you could be. As I remind every entrepreneur I coach or speak to, it's important to run your body like you run a business. You wouldn't take short cuts with your business, and you shouldn't do it with your body. After all, these two entities have a synergistic relationship.

Being a fit, happy, and productive entrepreneur requires a focus on more than your physical fitness. Our mental and emotional fitness play a pivotal role as well. Here are three simple but powerful tips to improve your mental and emotional fitness.

Don't Let Business Achievement Define You

In the beginning of your entrepreneurial journey, there isn't a raving fan club providing you validation. I was writing in obscurity for over a year before I received my first opportunity to write for a publication.

Entrepreneurs such as Daymond John, who many know as one of the judges on *Shark Tank*, worked for years in seeming obscurity. Years before he arrived on the scene, he was hustling on the streets while working at Red Lobster. If he had placed his identity 100 percent on the success of his business then, he wouldn't have lasted to become the success we know him as today.

As an entrepreneur, it's pivotal that you don't place your self-worth on the achievements of your business. At the start, it's important to be process oriented, not outcome oriented. You can only control the effort you put in each day, not the exact result or outcome it creates.

Understand that you're a human being who is separate from your business. The business may be your baby, but it doesn't dictate the currency of your self-worth. Take some time each day to reflect upon all the things you're proud of in your life.

Don't Allow Limiting Beliefs to Guide You

"I've never been good with fitness." "I'm too busy to exercise and eat clean." "My genetics don't allow me to lose weight." People actually believe such disempowering thoughts about themselves—even the most hard-driving, can-do businesspeople.

Maybe it's your past shortcomings or fear, but addressing the limiting beliefs that are circulating inside your brain is pivotal to improving your mental fitness as an entrepreneur.

Take some time to reflect on your beliefs. Where did these invisible scripts come from? Are they valid? Are these really your beliefs? Or are they beliefs programmed into you by external sources such as the media, family, peers or friends?

Don't Let Your Relationships Suffer

Your emotional fitness helps you manage, or even excel, amid the ups and downs of being an entrepreneur. With great emotional fitness comes a strong inner peace that allows you to stay connected to your true identity and make sound decisions for your business and health.

But, when you're running a business without a set number of hours and schedule, it's easy to lose focus on your emotional health. One key area for optimal emotional fitness is with those closest to us, whom we often push away without even noticing. It's not from lack of love; we often just take them for granted while becoming obsessed with our companies.

One of the simplest ways to enhance your business and health is to have powerful relationships, especially with your partner. It's pivotal to pick out a partner who understands your lifestyle and will be there to support you.

Knowing that you have a unique lifestyle and view of the world means that you can't just choose anyone as most people do. You have extra criteria that you have to be watchful for. While this may shrink your pool of potential partners, it provides a better chance of having a successful and powerful relationship that enriches you instead of draining you.

Instead of keeping your spouse or significant other in the dark about your business, let them into your world. Set aside time to focus on connection with them and nothing else. Plan for holidays and weekly date nights, making sure to mark them on the calendar.

It takes a lot of energy, strength, and dedication to start and grow a successful business. But you can't do this without focusing on your emotional and mental fitness. Your health equals your wealth.

WORK TO INGRAIN GRATITUDE INTO YOUR COMPANY CULTURE

Zeynep Ilgaz

Gratitude isn't something all of us talk about often in our workplace. We're busy building and running our companies, and it can be easy to forget to appreciate the people around us. This might seem like an innocent oversight—on the surface, there doesn't appear to be much of a correlation between gratitude and business success.

Yet science tells a different story.

Without gratitude, our teams might literally and figuratively fall apart. A 2015 study by the University of Montana confirmed that "grateful experiences and expressions" produce a positive impact on our psychological and physical well-being. Gratitude can even affect how well we sleep. According to a 2009 study in the *Journal of Psychosomatic Research*, people surveyed who said they'd expressed gratitude more frequently than average slept better and longer than those who expressed it less often.

This makes sense. After all, it's easy to see how a company's culture might diminish over time due to an absence of gratitude. Employees might grow dissatisfied and feel unmotivated, and innovation might grind to a halt. Job stress and turnover might become real concerns, and if these problems became epidemic, companies might well have problems bouncing back.

I've seen this happen firsthand. Before launching Confirm Biosciences, I worked for a fast-paced startup where everything was about hitting sales goals and making the board happy. Gratitude was the furthest thing from people's minds; employee recognition was seen as a waste of time. Believe it or not, even with such an emphasis on hitting goals and driving revenue, that company went out of business.

I promised myself back then that I would never let numbers or financial goals get in the way of gratitude, and I urge you to make the same promise to yourself.

The Business of Gratitude

Gratitude is more than just a simple "thanks" or "job well done." According to Globoforce, in 2014 a mere four percent of workers find these generic, nonspecific expressions of recognition memorable. So, when I speak of gratitude, I mean thoughtful, meaningful, and personalized acknowledgements. Your words and actions must show the recipient you truly recognize and appreciate his or her specific contributions.

I'd even argue that gratitude must become a cultural priority for your company. Why? Because according to a 2015 article from the *Harvard Business Review*, positive cultures foster productive workplaces. Appreciation is contagious, but in order to start this chain reaction of positivity and productivity, you—as the leader—need to be the role model. A culture of gratitude must begin at the top. Once your team members see you embody gratitude to your core, they will follow suit.

All told, a team that expresses and experiences gratitude doesn't just feel more motivated at work; it feels more appreciation for life. Sure, employees work harder and go above and beyond to innovate, but they also gain a greater sense of self-worth and self-efficacy.

So how do you get the gratitude ball rolling? The following steps are a good place to start:

1. Practice Makes Perfect

Habits—both good and bad—take time to form. According to a 2009 article from PsychCentral, it could take more than two months to cement a new behavior into your brain.

Gratitude is no exception to this rule. While it might feel unnatural to schedule a "gratitude reminder" in your calendar, doing so will help make it a natural part of your daily routine.

Then, to make it a natural part of your team's day, consider creating gratitude-focused activities and benefits at your business. At our company, we have something called a "gratitude box." Employees are encouraged to write and submit notes of gratitude about one other, and the team member with the most acknowledgements each month becomes employee of the month, a title that comes with a gift card to a store or restaurant the recipient personally enjoys.

2. Make It a Team Effort

There's an ongoing disconnect in the employee-recognition realm. According to a 2012 Bersin &

Associates study, only 58 percent of employees surveyed said their employers have recognition programs, even though three out of four companies surveyed said otherwise. What's more, just 17 percent of participants felt that their employers supported recognition.

Why is this happening? Gratitude, as they say, is in the eye of the beholder. If you have a culturally diverse team, you can be sure your employees all have different definitions of the words "appreciation" and "recognition." So ask your employees how they wish to be thanked and what it means to be appreciated. This will ensure that your gratitude resonates in relevant ways for everyone.

Next, consider following Zappos' lead by instilling peer-to-peer recognition programs that encourage your employees to express gratitude toward each other in creative ways. At the end of the day, you want meaningful displays of appreciation to flow throughout your company from a variety of sources.

3. Focus on Quality Over Quantity

According to a 2018 study published in the *Harvard Business Review,* a whopping 82 percent of American employees surveyed said they didn't feel recognized by leadership for their contributions at work. This alone should make you want to take a lap around the office to show some gratitude to your staff.

But before you head out, don't forget that quality always trumps quantity. One thoughtful gesture of gratitude is infinitely more powerful than 1,000 generic expressions of "thanks."

Just saying "great job" does not mean much if you fail to give a reason why. Be specific. Cite examples of how each team member is directly helping the company thrive. Show your employees that you see the connection between their contributions and your bottom line.

As humans, we have so much to be grateful for—and in our personal lives, these feelings come quite naturally to us. In the workplace, however, they can easily get lost in the day-to-day hustle of entrepreneurship.

So, make room for gratitude on your to-do list, and turn it into a cultural priority. Your employees will appreciate it and will work harder because of it. Ultimately, your business will be better off.

ENTREPRENEUR VOICES SPOTLIGHT: JARIE BOLANDER

Author and Tech Entrepreneur

With 20-plus years' experience in the Silicon Valley tech industry, including at six startups, Jarie Bolander had confronted numerous crises and near disasters over the years. He's seen first-hand the importance of solid values, traits, and beliefs in shaping both individuals and the companies they run.

In his book, *The Entrepreneur Ethos*, Bolander chronicles valuable lessons he and other entrepreneurs have learned over the years, including the importance high emotional intelligence plays in helping you stay nimble and flexible in the face of really nasty challenges.

Entrepreneur: You write that "without first overcoming our own fears, uncertainties, and doubts, we won't ever have the courage to start and carry on our life's work." Explain that.

Bolander: The most important thing you can control is yourself. Most of the time the challenges and struggles we have are all internal. It's how we react to the external world, how we deal with setbacks and challenges, that goes a long way in helping us figure out how to be emotionally stable. The people who I have seen with the highest amount of emotional intelligence know themselves, know what sets them off, and understand that they have to self-regulate. They believe in themselves, but they're not cocky. They don't think they know everything. Instead, they have the awareness to do things that calm them down when situations arise that are complex or difficult. They don't immediately lash out or point fingers at someone else. They try to empathize with and understand the problem. And if they don't have the answer, they are self-aware enough to know this and seek help from others.

Entrepreneur: Can you nurture yourself to have a higher EQ?

Bolander: Yes, I think you can nurture EQ, but a lot of it also depends on how much adversity and failure you've had to confront in your life. When I was growing up playing on sports teams, there were always winners and losers. We didn't get trophies just for showing up. For this reason, I learned fast that some days are just not my day. That doesn't mean that I'm a loser; it just means I need to try to do better next time. To nurture your EQ, you need to realize that failure is an option but never an end result. You need to recognize that bumps in the road are just setbacks. You need to look at failure as just a way to solve a problem, rather than dwelling on the unfairness of the situation.

Entrepreneur: You write a lot about integrity. How does that play into success?

Bolander: People with high EQ have a high sense of integrity. They know they need to seek the truth. When you are well-adjusted and sure of yourself, you truly understand that the truth will set you free. People who have high EQ understand that there are just some things that they can't change, but they have enough integrity to know that they may be wrong or need to change their opinion. They have enough tenacity to keep going even when things are not going their way. A lot of people quit too early. High EQers have a bendable way that they can go through the world. They bend instead of break. They're loose.

Entrepreneur: How do you know when it's time to quit?

Bolander: If I'm not making progress, then I know that's a signal it may be time to stop. And by progress—I mean both positive and negative progress. You can be going backward and that's still progress. At least you're moving in some direction. You just need to pivot and readjust. The worst is when I'm stagnant in my business for a while, and I'm not moving forward, then I know it's time to quit.

PART IV
MAINTAINING YOUR EQ— REFLECTIONS

Emotions have an important place in business. You don't want to lead like some sort of unsympathetic robot. At the same time, unchecked emotions and feelings can stand in the way of success. Those who manage their feelings like mature adults rather than impetuous teens will feel a lot better about themselves, and they'll inspire others to do the same.

So how does one manage his emotions? You can start by observing your own emotional experience as a spectator rather than a participant. No judgment. No resistance. Just sit with the feelings, be objective, and act without reacting.

Good emotional managers excel at self-control and staying calm in the face of negativity. They're unfazed by rejection and the word "no" because they see it as an opportunity to get closer to "yes." They know when to ask for help or take time for themselves.

The ability to manage our emotions takes practice and hard work. You must develop this talent like you would a muscle or a certain athletic skill, practicing regularly and not being afraid to fail. As Ice Cube once said, you need to "check yourself before you wreck yourself."

RESOURCES

(in order of appearance)

Thank you to our talented Entrepreneur contributors whose content is featured in this book. For more information about these contributors, including author bios, visit us at www.entrepreneur.com.

1. Gerard Adams, "What is emotional intelligence and Why Does it Matter?" *Entrepreneur*, May 13, 2016, http://entrepreneur.com/article/275348.

2. Travis Bradberry, "11 Signs That You Lack emotional intelligence," *Entrepreneur*, January 24, 2017, http://entrepreneur.com/article/299452.

3. Mariah DeLeon, "The Importance of emotional intelligence at Work," *Entrepreneur*, May 8, 2015, http://entrepreneur.com/article/245755.

4. Jonathan Long, "Are You Self-Aware? 5 Key Traits You Need to Have to Be a Great Entrepreneur." *Entrepreneur*, October 30, 2017, http://entrepreneur.com/article/303797.

5. Jayson DeMers, "5 Signs You're Too Emotional to Decide What's Best for Your Business," *Entrepreneur*, August 22, 2016, http://entrepreneur.com/article/281160.

6. Mary Deelsnyder, "Why Vulnerability, Authenticity and Love Are 3 Must-Haves for Entrepreneurs," *Entrepreneur*, February 12, 2017, http://entrepreneur.com/article/270702.

7. Jayson DeMers, "7 Signs That You're an Emotionally Intelligent Person," *Entrepreneur*, May 11, 2017, http://entrepreneur.com/article/293826.

8. Ray Hennessey, "Embrace the Imperfect Picture Beneath Your Masterpiece," *Entrepreneur*,

December 8, 2015, http://entrepreneur.com/article/253729.

9. Anis Qizilbash, "4 Ways to Tame Your Negativity Bias," *Entrepreneur*, July 25, 2016, http://entrepreneur.com/article/279044.

10. Jim Joseph, "Cut People a Break. You Never Know What They're Going Through." *Entrepreneur*, February 3, 2016, http://entrepreneur.com/article/270227.

11. Travis Bradberry, "9 Signs You're Dealing with an Emotional Manipulator," *Entrepreneur*, November 29, 2016, http://entrepreneur.com/article/285780.

12. Travis Bradberry, "8 Great Tricks for Reading People's Body Language," *Entrepreneur*, May 18, 2016, http://entrepreneur.com/article/299722.

13. Jason Wesbecher, "How the New Emotional Workplace Affects Hiring, Retention and Culture," *Entrepreneur*, May 9, 2016, http://entrepreneur.com/article/272914.

14. Tracy Maylett, "8 Solutions for Managing a Passive-Aggressive Team," *Entrepreneur*, November 13, 2017, http://entrepreneur.com/article/300819.

15. Ivan Misner, "Be Self-Aware, Be Selfless, and Then Be Selfish," *Entrepreneur*, September 30, 2015, http://entrepreneur.com/article/251173.

16. Nathan Chan, "How to Use Emotional Decision-Making in Marketing," *Entrepreneur*, February 3, 2017, http://entrepreneur.com/article/288512.

17. Kevin Xu, "Managing Your Mental Health as an Entrepreneur," *Entrepreneur*, January 5, 2017, http://entrepreneur.com/article/285854.

18. David Osborn, "4 Ways to Overcome Grief Without Neglecting Your Business," *Entrepreneur*, January 19, 2017, http://entrepreneur.com/article/286775.

19. Dan Steiner, "4 Tips for Entrepreneurial Survival During the Grieving Process," *Entrepreneur*, December 1, 2015, http://entrepreneur.com/article/252991.

20. Jayson DeMers, "The 5 Biggest Psychological Hurdles of Entrepreneurship," *Entrepreneur*, February 4, 2016, http://entrepreneur.com/article/269883.

21. Ray Hennessey, "Don't Let the Loneliness of Entrepreneurship Kill You," *Entrepreneur*, January 5, 2016, http://entrepreneur.com/article/254641.

22. Ray Hennessey, "Believing You're Capable Demands Doubting Yourself," *Entrepreneur*, October 12, 2015, http://entrepreneur.com/article/251630.

23. Lena Requist, "How to Develop a Positive Relationship with Failure," *Entrepreneur*, September 25, 2017, http://entrepreneur.com/article/300563.

24. Graham Young, "How to Be Grateful When Times Are Tough," *Entrepreneur*, January 21, 2017, http://entrepreneur.com/article/254199.

25. Sherrie Campbell, "9 Practices for Achieving Emotional Maturity," *Entrepreneur*, September 22, 2016, http://entrepreneur.com/article/282654.

26. Adam Toren, "7 Things Grandpa Joe Taught My Brother and Me About Entrepreneurship," *Entrepreneur*, January 19, 2017, http://entrepreneur.com/article/287626.

27. Barrett Wissman, "10 Ways to Motivate Yourself When You're Really Not Feeling It," *Entrepreneur*, November 3, 2017, http://entrepreneur.com/article/304031.

28. Sherrie Campbell, "7 Emotional Management Practices that Propel Success," *Entrepreneur*,

August 25, 2016, http://entrepreneur.com/article/281339.

29. Deep Patel, "10 Ways to Become a Super-Likable Person," *Entrepreneur*, April 28, 2017, http://entrepreneur.com/article/293343.

30. Sherrie Campbell, "5 Ways Criticism and Rejection Builds Your Capacity to Succeed," *Entrepreneur*, June 25, 2015, http://entrepreneur.com/article/247634.

31. Julian Hayes II, "3 Powerful Tips to Improve Your Emotional and Mental Fitness," *Entrepreneur*, February 13, 2017, http://entrepreneur.com/article/288767.

32. Zeynep Ilgaz, "Where's the Love? Why You Should Work to Ingrain Gratitude Into Your Company Culture," *Entrepreneur*, September 6, 2017, http://entrepreneur.com/article/299120.

Reader's Notes

DISCOVER AND ACHIEVE YOUR FULL POTENTIAL WITH THE ENTREPRENEUR VOICES SERIES

Entrepreneur Voices on Effective Leadership
ISBN 978-1-59918-617-7
entm.ag/voicesonleadership

Entrepreneur Voices on Strategic Management
ISBN 978-1-59918-618-4
entm.ag/voicesonmanagement

Entrepreneur Voices on Company Culture
ISBN 978-1-59918-626-9
entm.ag/voicesoncompanyculture

Entrepreneur Voices on Growth Hacking
ISBN 978-1-59918-627-6
entm.ag/voicesongrowthhacking

AVAILABLE WHEREVER BOOKS AND EBOOKS ARE SOLD

CPSIA information can be obtained
at www.ICGtesting.com
Printed in the USA
JSHW011937240423
40756JS00010B/913